Human Resource Management Practices

Human Resource Management Practices

A Biblical Perspective

MONICA SIFUNA-EVELIA

PARTRIDGE

Print information available on the last page.

To order additional copies of this book, contact
Toll Free 800 101 2657 (Singapore)
Toll Free 1 800 81 7340 (Malaysia)
orders.singapore@partridgepublishing.com

www.partridgepublishing.com/singapore

CONTENTS

"Human Resources is not a thing we do. It's the thing that runs our business."

Steve Wynn

DEDICATION

To my husband Paul and son Jabari

ACKNOWLEDGEMENT

I want to thank God Almighty for seeing me through this and keeping me motivated. In addition, I wish to thank my family; my husband, Mr. Paul Evelia, for supporting me in my quest for writing a book; my dad, Mr. Peter Musumba Sifuna for always telling me that I can achieve anything that I put my mind to do; my mum, Ms. Mwanahawa Sarah Shisia for always believing in me; Reverend Fr. Fredrick Mukabana of the Roman Catholic Church for proof-reading the book and giving me guidance in the writing process; Senior Pastor John Wesley Nguuh of CITAM Eldoret for giving me the drive I needed to take the leap; and Mr. Godfrey Ombogo for editing the book.

1.0 RECRUITMENT

Recruitment refers to the overall process of attracting, selecting and appointing suitable candidates for jobs (either permanent or temporary) within an organization. The recruitment process highlighted here is in relation to the Employment Act 2007.

1.1 Manpower planning

Manpower planning is about forecasting staff requirements versus availability of staff. It is prudent to plan for staff needs at the beginning of the year. When a human resource practitioner plans for staff requirements he/she will be able to enjoy benefits such as identifying shortages and surpluses and taking quick action; base all recruitment and selection on the manpower planning; reduce labor costs; identify available talent among staff; and initiate growth and diversification of business. The book of Proverbs 21:5 states "The plans of the diligent lead to profit as surely as haste leads to poverty."

The Gospel of Luke emphasizes the importance of being prepared and steadfast at all times. "But stay awake at all times, praying that you may have strength to escape all these things that are going to take place and to stand before the Son of Man." (Luke 21:36).

A cost-benefit analysis example is given by Jesus when he tells his disciples of one having to sit down and do a cost-benefit analysis before building a tower. "Suppose one of you wants to build a tower. Won't you first sit down and estimate the cost to see if you have enough money to complete it? For if you lay the foundation and are not able to finish it, everyone who sees it will ridicule you, saying, 'This person began to build and wasn't able to finish.'"(Luke 14:28-30). While projecting staffing needs, a human resource practitioner is expected to look at the economic viability of the projection. There is need to know how to get the revenue that will go to the staffing costs. A human resource practitioner, therefore, will look at options such as having staff on casual basis who can perform tasks on a wage rate to help cut down the cost of other benefits such as medical cover, annual leave, among others. In my experience in the security and health industries, we have explored the use of casual staff to cut staffing costs.

In one of my experiences at the health facility, I earned myself a seat at the implementation of a strategic plan for the period 2015-2019. In the strategic plan, different activities were slotted to be achieved in different years. We had activities that had to be done in 2015, others 2017 and so on and so forth. At the end of every year, we would sit down as management team and go through the activities for the year, looking at those we were able to accomplish and those we were not. Challenges in this implementation would also be highlighted and recommendations for better results obtained.

A human resource practitioner is expected to forecast the need for staffing and prepare for the same, considering the revision of wage rate and the market rate for similar positions in the industry. In another experience at the health facility, we set aside a budget for miscellaneous just in case the government implemented the Collective Bargaining Agreement that the Kenya Medical Practitioners and Dentists Union had been asking for. Doctors in Kenya had been on strike from December 2016 to February 2017 over their salaries. We knew as management that should the government implement the Collective Bargaining Agreement then we would have to adjust our doctors' salaries to enhance employee retention. In the Gospel of Mathew, disciples asked Jesus on the Mount of Olives about the sign of his coming in reference to preparedness. "As he sat on the Mount of Olives, the disciples came to him privately, saying, "Tell us, when will these things be, and what will be the sign of your coming and of the close of the age?"(Matthew 24:3).

In the same Gospel, we are advised on the importance of staying awake as we await the coming of our Lord. "Therefore, stay awake; for you do not know on what day your Lord is coming." (Matthew 24:42).

A Human Resource Plan needs to be in place, one has to forecast the manpower needs and to compare it with the current supply of manpower in order to determine the next course of action. This plan has to be in line with the overall strategic plan of the organization. The human resource practitioner will look at where the organization is aiming to be in the next financial year, and see if these needs will be met by the current manpower or there will be need to recruit. If an organization for instance is introducing a new product, there might be need to source for staff with particular skills to suit the needs of the new business.

In my experience, I have always prepared a human resource management plan at the beginning of every year. Management would hold a meeting at the beginning of every year where all managers would present the plans in their respective functions in the institution.

When the demand for manpower is higher than the supply the human resource practitioner can explore options like recruitment; multitasking, job rotation and job enhancement. On the other hand, when the supply of manpower is higher than the demand he/she can explore options like retrenchment; freezing recruitment, early retirement and redundancy.

In the security company, at one point we got a big contract to provide security services to a cement manufacturing site in Mombasa. We therefore recruited over 200 security officers for this client. When I was in the media industry, we did a restructuring and laid off a number of staff. The staff who remained were mandated to multitask such that one would be a television show host and a producer concurrently.

In the health facility, we performed job rotation for our nurses after every six months. The nurses would rotate in the various departments in the hospital such as Outpatient, Maternity Ward, Pediatric Ward, Medical Ward, Surgical Ward, Child Welfare Clinic and Antenatal Clinic.

1.2 Recruitment process

The process starts from the time a position is declared vacant up to when it is filled. When a position falls vacant, it is the responsibility of the line manager to identify the need to recruit based on increased workload; organizational change; staff movement; technological changes and positions falling vacant due to resignation, termination, dismissal, transfer or promotion. The process described below is as I have experienced in the various industries that I have worked in.

The human resource practitioner will raise the staff requisition form, attaching a job description, and forward it to the Chief Executive Officer for appropriate authorization. The Chief Executive Officer will review and approve the staff requisition. Upon approval, the human resource practitioner will prepare a job advertisement for either internally or externally using appropriate means. The human resource practitioner will receive applications; do initial shortlist and forward to respective line managers for further shortlisting whilst acknowledging applications at the earliest opportunity. Once the shortlist is done, interview invites are done at least two days before the interview date. The human resource practitioner prepares interview questions and organizes for the interviews. The interview panel encompasses the human resource practitioner and the relevant line manager.

The interview feedback is then given. Regret is sent to the unsuccessful candidates and the successful ones are informed of the documentation that they are supposed to bring when reporting. (2 recent color passport size photographs; an updated copy of the CV; a copy of all the certificates as listed on the CV; a copy of the national ID; a copy of the NHIF card; a copy of the NSSF card; a copy of the KRA Pin Certificate; and bank details (copy of the ATM card) and bank branch).

On the reporting day, the human resource practitioner receives the new employee and does the initial induction. The new employee is issued with a job description and deployed in their respective department for a thorough induction.

Once the new employee has reported, induction is organized. Usually the induction schedule is prepared. The general induction is done by the human resource practitioner who then hands over the staff to the head of department. The human resource practitioner would take the new staff through the employee code of conduct, the human resource policies, and the staff manual and physical orientation in the organization. The head of department will usually have a detailed induction schedule. Both the new staff and the head of department will sign the induction schedule and return it to the human resource department for filing.

The book of Nehemiah gives a good example on recruitment policies where men are given the responsibilities over the provisions which were offered for worship in the Temple. "On that day men were also appointed over the chambers for the stores, the contributions, the first fruits and the tithes, to gather into them from the fields of the cities the portions required by the law for the priests and Levites; for Judah rejoiced over the priests and Levites who served."(Nehemiah 12:44).

Human resource practitioners are supposed to treat all employees equally and fairly. The Employment Act 2007 Section 5 warns against discrimination in employment. The law mandates Labor Officers and the Industrial Court to promote equality of opportunity in employment in order to eliminate discrimination in employment; and to promote and guarantee equality of opportunity for a person, who is a migrant worker or a member of the family of the migrant worker, lawfully within Kenya. It mandates an employer to promote equal opportunity in employment and strive to eliminate discrimination in any employment policy or practice. No employer is to discriminate, directly or indirectly, against an employee or prospective employee or harass an employee or prospective employee—on grounds of race, color, sex, language, religion, political or other opinion, nationality, ethnic or social origin, disability, pregnancy, mental status or HIV status; in respect of recruitment, training, promotion, terms and conditions of employment, termination of employment or other matters arising out of the employment.

In the various industries where I have worked, we have always derived the Equal Opportunities Policy from the above clause. The book of Leviticus 25:53 gives instructions to employers on how to treat the workers who are hired on yearly basis by not ruling over them ruthlessly. "...they are to be treated as workers hired from year to year; you must see to it that those to whom they owe service do not rule over them ruthlessly." (Leviticus 25:53).

According to the book of 2 Chronicles, King Solomon made good preparations before commencing to build the Temple where the Lord would be worshipped. "I am sending you Hiram-Abi, a man of great skill, whose mother was from Dan and whose father was from Tyre. He is trained to work in gold and silver, bronze and iron, stone and wood, and with purple and blue and crimson yarn and fine linen. He is experienced in all kinds of engraving and can execute any design given to him. He will work with your skilled workers and with those of my lord, David your father." (2 Chronicles 2: 13-14). At the health facility, at some point there was expansion of services. The hospital introduced a Critical Care Unit and Dialysis. This had been projected in the Strategic Plan of 2015-2019. The hospital therefore had sponsored three nurses to go and study Critical Care Nursing and Nephrology in anticipation of this expansion. These nurses were to be the pioneers of the two departments as we continued to recruit other skilled nurses in the two specialties.

The book of Proverbs 26:10 warns us against the temptation of just hiring any passersby. This reiterates the importance of having job requirements. "…Like an archer who wounds at random is one who hires a fool or any passer-by." (Proverbs 26:10) It is important to have job requirements that a candidate must meet in the recruitment process. In the various industries I have worked, I have experienced demands from managers fronting resumes for consideration for employment from their persons of interest. It is a sad situation in cases where the manager giving you those demands is, in fact, your immediate supervisor and the resume does not meet the qualifications for the job advertised. This then puts a human resource practitioner in a dilemma since the policies are supposed to be adhered to as designed. More often than not, you will find such persons failing to perform the tasks given to them.

Prophet Isaiah talks of how all the hired laborers were grieved in their souls following the crushing of the Pillars of Egypt as a punishment from God and how the weavers and skilled workers were broken and depressed. This is an indication that recruitments of laborers were done as early as in the era of the prophets. "And the Pillars of Egypt will be crushed; all the hired laborers will be grieved in soul." (Isaiah 19:10).

Division of labor is one of the vital elements of an organization as a function of management. In every working set-up, there are different roles to be performed by different employees. This is covered in their job description. There are also tasks that are supposed to be handled by a manager but may be delegated to another staff in cases where the manager is absent or preoccupied with another task. This is clearly seen in the book of Exodus where we encounter a scenario of Moses receiving instructions from his father-in-law to select capable men from all the people and have them serve as Judges for the people at all times.

"...But select capable men from all the people—men who fear God, trustworthy men who hate dishonest gain—and appoint them as officials over thousands, hundreds, fifties and tens. Have them serve as judges for the people at all times, but have them bring every difficult case to you; the simple cases they can decide themselves." (Exodus 18:21-22).

When I took a job at the health facility, I was tasked to set up a human resource management office and run it. One of my tasks was to prepare job descriptions for all positions in the hospital in conjunction with the heads of departments. The positions included nurses, doctors, clinical officers, support staff, receptionists, health records staff, anesthetists, cashiers, chaplaincy, among others.

Division of labor is clearly brought out in 1Chronicles "...David left Asaph and his associates before the ark of the covenant of the LORD to minister there regularly, according to each day's requirements. He also left Obed-Edom and his sixty-eight associates to minister with them. Obed-Edom son of Jeduthun, and also Hosah, were gatekeepers. David left Zadok the priest and his fellow priests before the tabernacle of the LORD at the high place in Gibeon to present burnt offerings to the LORD on the altar of burnt offering regularly, morning and evening, in accordance with everything written in the Law of the LORD, which he had given Israel. With them were Heman and Jeduthun and the rest of those chosen and designated by name to give thanks to the LORD, "or his love endures forever.' Heman and Jeduthun were responsible for the sounding of the trumpets and cymbals and for the playing of the other instruments for sacred song. The sons of Jeduthun were stationed at the gate." (1Chronicles16: 37-42); and 18:14: "David reigned over all Israel, doing what was just and right for all his people. Joab son of Zeruiah was over the army; Jehoshaphat son of Ahilud was a recorder; Zadokson of Ahitub and Ahimelek son of Abiathar were priests; Shavsha was secretary; Benaiah son of Jehoiada was over the Kerethites and Pelethites; and David's sons were chief officials at the king's side."

In the media company we had video editors, news reporters, sub-editors, support staff, accountants, sales persons, radio presenters, television anchors, among others. 2 Chronicles 24:12, indicates that the king and Jehoiada hired masons and carpenters to restore the LORD's temple, and also workers in iron and bronze to repair the temple. "The king and Jehoiada gave it to those who carried out the work required for the temple of the LORD. They hired masons and carpenters to restore the LORD's temple, and also workers in iron and bronze to repair the temple." In (2 Chronicles 25:6), the king also hired a hundred thousand fighting men from Israel for a hundred talents of silver.

At one point when I was working at the health facility, construction was going on as per the expansion plan. We hired a clerk of works to oversee the construction. The clerk of works had laborers in various fields such as plumbing, electrical engineering, carpentry, and welding. In the media company, I was in charge of a renovation project for floor tiles and washrooms of the entire organization. I sourced for quotations from suppliers and selected the person who did the job together with his team of laborers. In the same company, I was also in charge of ensuring all lights and desks for employees were in good working condition. I would from time to time hire casual workers in electrical engineering and carpentry to come and fix the lights and desks. David tells Solomon that he has many workers. He says, "You have many workers: stonecutters, masons and carpenters, as well as those skilled in every kind of work in gold and silver, bronze and iron—craftsmen beyond number. Now begin the work, and the LORD be with you." (1Chronicles 22:15). He continues to say, "Of these, twenty-four thousand are to be in charge of the work of the temple of the LORD and six thousand are to be officials and judges. Four thousand are to be gatekeepers and four thousand are to praise the LORD with the musical instruments I have provided for that purpose." David separated the Levites into divisions corresponding to the sons of Levi: Gershon, Kohath and Merari. According to the last instructions of David, the Levites were counted from those twenty years old or more. The duty of the Levites was to help Aaron's descendants in the service of the temple of the LORD: to be in charge of the courtyards, the side rooms, the purification of all sacred things and the performance of other duties at the house of God. They were in charge of the bread set out on the table, the special flour for the grain offerings, the thin loaves made without yeast, the baking and the mixing, and all measurements of quantity and size. They were also to stand every morning to thank and praise the LORD. They were to do the same in the evening and whenever burnt offerings were presented to the LORD on the Sabbaths, at the New Moon feasts and at the appointed festivals. They were to serve before the LORD regularly in the proper number and in the way prescribed for them. And so the Levites carried out their responsibilities for the tent of meeting, for the Holy Place and, under their relatives the descendants of Aaron, for the service of the temple of the LORD.(1 Chronicle 23:4-32).

When I was working in the security company, I was the chairperson of the Health and Safety Committee for eight branches of the company. I therefore delegated my role to the branch managers of the eight branches because I could not be in all places at the same time. I tasked the branch managers to appoint a health and safety committee within their respective branches. They were to hold monthly meetings, conduct a health and safety audit, identify hazards, perform a risk assessment, and sensitize all staff on health and safety matters. 2 Chronicles: 2:1-9 states, "Solomon gave orders to build a temple for the Name of the LORD and a royal palace for himself. He conscripted 70,000 men as carriers and 80,000 as stonecutters in the hills and 3,600 as foremen over them. He advertised a job for a man skilled to work in gold and silver, bronze and iron, and in purple, crimson and blue yarn, and experienced in the art of engraving, to work in Judah and Jerusalem with my skilled workers, whom my father David provided. He also advertised for a cedar, juniper and algum logs from Lebanon, the servants were skilled in cutting timber there."

When a human resource practitioner is putting up a job advertisement using various channels, he/she must ensure that the advertisement has presented the job requirements as expected. The job requirements will cover the academic qualifications and the personal attributes of the candidate. The book of 1Timothy gives us the job requirements of a church leader and church helpers. "...This is a true saying: If a man is eager to be a church leader, he desires an excellent work. A church leader must be without fault; he must have only one wife, be sober, self-controlled, and orderly; he must welcome strangers in his home; he must be able to teach; he must not be a drunkard or a violent man, but gentle and peaceful; he must not love money; he must be able to manage his own family well and make his children obey him with all respect. For if a man does not know how to manage his own family, how can he take care of the church of God? He must be mature in the faith, so that he will not swell up with pride and be condemned, as the Devil was. He should be a man who is respected by the people outside the church, so that he will not be disgraced and fall into the Devil's trap. Church helpers must also have a good character and be sincere; they must not drink too much wine or be greedy for money; they should hold to the revealed truth of the faith with a clear conscience. They should be tested first, and then, if they pass the test, they are to serve. Their wives also must be of good character and must not gossip; they must be sober and honest in everything. A church helper must have only one wife, and be able to manage his children and family well. Those helpers who do their work well win for themselves a good standing and are able to speak boldly about their faith in Christ Jesus."(1Timothy 3:1-13).

The book of 2 Timothy speaks of people recruiting teachers for them to suit their own passions. This is what happens when you hire someone for the wrong reasons. In the day-to-day life you see managers in the name of bosses promising employment to people in exchange for favors, such that someone is not really hired because of their qualifications. "... For the time is coming when people will not endure sound teaching, but having itching ears they will accumulate for themselves teachers to suit their own passions, and will turn away from listening to the truth and wander off into myths."

(2 Timothy 4:3-4).

Some of the challenges I have experienced in the recruitment process include managers going against the recruitment policy. For example, for academic qualifications, where a subordinate staff position requires at least a KCSE certificate, you will find a manager bringing the names of candidates with only KCPE certificates for consideration. Human resource practitioners also get pressure from managers to recruit specific persons for their own vested interests; for instance, people from their communities who may or may not meet job requirements. We also face situations where the top management gives instructions to freeze recruitment even when there is budget for the said position. Top management sometimes, in the spirit of cost cutting, recommends the use of temporary staffs that end up exceeding the three months limit required by law. The other challenge is having candidates who lie about their capabilities in interviews and fail to perform when recruited, among others.

When I was working in the security company, there was a time we got a big contract to supply security services at a refugee camp in Kakuma, Turkana County. I got a lot of challenges from the community elders, politicians and supervisors. The branch manager was at some point threatened that this was their land and he must recruit from the community. Recruitment therefore became a political and community affair and ceased to follow the requirements for the job. Some of the job requirements that were overlooked were the academic qualifications and a person's height. The politicians would send a list of the persons to be hired; the security supervisors within the company would also front their lists. When I became strict on the job requirements, we got a threat to nullify the entire recruitment and take away the contract. In my case I wrote a recruitment report and forwarded to my Human Resource Director who gave me further instructions.

1.3 Induction

Induction refers to the process of orientation of a new staff. This is usually done after the staff has been given an offer letter and has reported to work.

The Bible indicates in various texts that once you have recruited a staff, it is important to give them orientation/induction into the work place and overall organization's culture. A new staff will be required to embrace the organization's culture and learn the various services and products of the company. The new staff will be required to read and understand the employee code of conduct and the organization's policies.

According to the book of Ezra, Ezra received instructions to appoint magistrates and judges and teach those that do not know the laws of God. "...And you, Ezra, in accordance with the wisdom of your God, which you possess, appoint magistrates and judges to administer justice to all the people of Trans-Euphrates—all who know the laws of your God. And you are to teach any who do not know them."(Ezra 7:25). While working for a manufacturing company, we recruited casuals who were to work in the workshop where machines were running. We appointed a supervisor to lead them into a two-week induction where they were trained on how to operate the machines, wearing their personal protective equipment at all times and reporting of any health and safety incidences. This is also as guided by the Occupational Health and Safety Act of 2007 Section 6, which states that it is the duty of the employer to provide information, instruction, training and supervision as is necessary to ensure the safety and health at work of every person employed.

The book of Thessalonians gives us an example where Paul asks the believers if they remembered what he told them when he was with them. "Let no one deceive you in any way. For that day will not come, unless the rebellion comes first, and the man of lawlessness is revealed, the son of destruction, who opposes and exalts himself against every so-called god or object of worship, so that he takes his seat in the temple of God, proclaiming himself to be God. Do you not remember that when I was still with you I told you these things? And you know what is restraining him now so that he may be revealed in his time. For the mystery of lawlessness is already at work. Only he who now restrains it will do so until he is out of the way." (2 Thessalonians 2:3-8). This verse shows that once induction has taken place, the employee is supposed to ascertain that they have undergone the induction.

In the media company and health facility where I worked, I always prepared an induction schedule which has several sections of the induction program. The induction program would have a place where the human resource practitioner, the line manager and the new employee would append their signatures. A copy of the induction schedule is kept in the employees' personal file.

Some of the problems that employees and employers face stem from not having proper orientation. Some staff would say they have no idea who the new staff is. In the media company, there was a new staff in ICT department who had been sent to fix the laptop of a senior manager. These two had never met. The senior manager almost called security to report a stranger in his office. In the health facility, there was a problem with a receptionist at the Radiography department. The head of department came to me to report that the staff was underperforming. Upon doing my investigations, I found out that the staff was not orientated into the new job; she had worked as a receptionist in a different department within the very facility where roles were slightly different. I then instructed the head of department to prepare a thorough induction schedule; train the staff and bring me the signed copy. Since then, the head of department never complained of the receptionist's inefficiency again.

When I was working at the media company, once a new staff reported we would notify all staff and even send a photo of the new employee on email or on a notice board. I would then take the new staff round the organization and show him/her each office then hand them over to their head of department where proper and detailed departmental induction is also done.

1.4 Terms of service

Once a candidate has been found successful for a particular position, the terms of service are laid out. The Bible gives us a number of examples where terms of engagement were clearly outlined.

1.4.1 Hours of work

The Employment Act of 2007 Section 27 states that an employer shall regulate the working hours of each employee in accordance with the provisions of this Act and any other written law. An employee shall be entitled to at least one rest day in every period of seven days. According to the book of Exodus, God gave instruction to the Israelites to work for six days but rest so that their oxes and their donkeys may rest, and so that the workers in their households and the foreigners living among them may be refreshed. "…Six days do your work, but on the seventh day do not work, so that your ox and your donkey may rest, and so that the slave born in your household and the foreigner living among you may be refreshed." (Exodus 23:12).

At the health facility, we always had staff complaining over their working hours. We introduced a biometric machine to monitor employees' reporting time and attendance. When cautioned on late coming, the employees would say they compensated by working longer hours than what the Employment Act recommended. According to the Employment Act 2007, employees are supposed to work for eight hours per day. The medical staff would more often than not find themselves working for longer hours. A case in point are the doctors, anesthetists and nurses in theatre; ideally they are supposed to work for eight hours per day. But in the event that a surgery is ongoing in the theatre, they would not leave the operation half way just because their working hours have elapsed. These employees have used this scenario to request for overtime payment.

In the manufacturing company, the clock-in and clock-out system was used both ways as a discipline management and reward tool, such that when a staff is late the system flags them and when someone has worked for more hours, the extra hours are counted as overtime and they are subsequently paid for the same.

The same can be applied in cases of annual leave. The Employment Act 2007 Section 28 states that an employee shall be entitled—after every twelve consecutive months of service with his employer to not less than twenty-one working days of leave with full pay; where employment is terminated after the completion of two or more consecutive months of service during any twelve months' leave-earning period, to not less than one and three-quarter days of leave with full pay, in respect of each completed month of service in that period, to be taken consecutively. An employer may, with the consent of the employee, divide the minimum annual leave entitlement into different parts to be taken at different intervals. This helps to prevent burn out and to minimize employee stress levels and increase their productivity.

The Employment Act gives a guideline and in most cases is used as the minimum acceptable requirement. As such, different organizations would have different leave entitlements. For instance, at the media company, all staff were entitled to 21 working days. At the security company, senior management and middle-level managers were entitled to 24 working days while the frontline staffs were entitled to 30 calendar days translating to 26 working days.

According to the book of Exodus, Moses asked the Israelites to obey the Sabbath day and keep it holy. "Say to the Israelites, You must observe my Sabbaths. This will be a sign between me and you for the generations to come, so you may know that I am the LORD, who makes you holy. Observe the Sabbath, because it is holy to you. Anyone who desecrates it is to be put to death; those who do any work on that day must be cut off from their people. For six days work is to be done, but the seventh day is a day of Sabbath rest, holy to the LORD. Whoever does any work on the Sabbath day is to be put to death. The Israelites are to observe the Sabbath, celebrating it for the generations to come as a lasting covenant. It will be a sign between me and the Israelites forever, for in six days the LORD made the heavens and the earth, and on the seventh day he rested and was refreshed." (Exodus 31:12-17).

In the health facility and the security company, employees took their one day of rest at alternate times because of the shifts of work. In the security company, we had night and day shifts; while at the health facility we had the morning shift, straight shift, evening shift and night shift. In both organizations, employees' off-days would fall on different days, sometimes on a week day. At the media company, the one day of rest mostly fell on weekends because there was only one shift. Exodus 20:8-10 states, "Remember the Sabbath day, to keep it holy. Six days you shall labor, and do all your work, but the seventh day is a Sabbath to the Lord your God. On it you shall not do any work, you, or your son, or your daughter, your male servant, or your female servant, or your livestock, or the sojourner who is within your gates."

1.4.2 Job Description

When a new employee reports, a job description is among the documents that he/she receives at the human resource department. When I joined the health facility, I found out that not all employees had their job descriptions. I worked together with the various heads of departments and prepared job descriptions for all employees in the facility. Employees were given their copies and the other copies were kept in their personal files. According to the Gospel of Mark, Jesus gave his disciples instructions to go into the entire world and to proclaim the gospel to the whole creation. "Go into the entire world and proclaim the gospel to the whole creation." (Mark 16:14-16).

Staffs have in many occasions come to me to say they are doing work that is not supposed to be theirs. One of the gardeners at the health facility reported that he does more than gardening work and he wanted clarification on what his job description really should read. The Gospel of John gives us an instance where John the Baptist's job is described as having come as a witness, to bear witness about the light, that all might believe through him. "The light shines in the darkness, and the darkness has not overcome it. There was a man sent from God, whose name was John. He came as a witness, to bear witness about the light, that all might believe through him." (John 1:5-7).

A job description will usually indicate the job title, the department and the person that the employee will report to. The book of 1 Peter gives us an episode where workers are advised in reverent fear of God to submit themselves to their masters. "Slaves, in reverent fear of God, submit yourselves to your masters, not only to those who are good and considerate, but also to those who are harsh." (1 Peter 2:18).

A job description of a marketing officer in a health facility, for example, will highlight the duties as coming up with a marketing strategy for the hospital; increasing revenue through enrolling new corporate clients and consultants; coordinating events within the hospital as a revenue line; identifying marketing opportunities by identifying consumer requirements; improving product/service marketability and profitability by researching, identifying and capitalizing on market opportunities; enhancing social media presence of the hospital; identifying product/service improvements or new products/services by remaining current on industry trends, market activities and competitors; creating awareness of the hospital in the market for proper positioning; preparing promotional event flyers for hospital events; confirming with heads of departments on the upcoming events and posting them on the website and social media platforms; developing customer satisfaction programs; improving total quality of the hospital in liaison with other managers; ensuring awareness of the hospital events and services to the existing members; maintaining and updating information on the hospital's website; preparing and supervising the production of publicity brochures, handouts, direct meal leaflets, promotional videos, photographs, films and multimedia programs; and managing media and information dissemination.

According to the Gospel of Mathew, the disciples received instructions from Jesus prescribing their job description as he sent them to the mission in the whole world. "…Go therefore and make disciples of all nations, baptizing them in the name of the Father and of the Son and of the Holy Spirit." (Matthew 28:19).

A general manager's job description is to oversee the operations of the entire organization. The book of Genesis gives us an example of Adam being put in charge of the Garden of Eden. "The Lord God took the man and put him in the Garden of Eden to work it and take care of it."(Genesis 2:15).

Every job requires specific skills to perform. Some of the positions in a banking institution include credit controller, marketing executive, bank teller, financial analyst, human resource officer, public relations officer, personal assistant, receptionist and support staff. All these jobs require skills specific to each job. The book of Exodus gives us an example of various skills for performing various jobs as graces showered upon people from God. "He has filled them with skill to do all kinds of work as engravers, designers, embroiderers in blue, purple and scarlet yarn and fine linen, and weavers—all of them skilled workers and designers." (Exodus 35:35).

When I worked at a small advertising company, we had positions like creative director, graphic designers, video and content editors, advertising executives, administrator, general manager, accountant and office assistant. My job title was Advertising Executive and my role was to sell advertising space in two magazines; one targeting the high-end market and the other targeting the youth. The letter of St. Paul to the Ephesians gives an instance fitting the allocations of various job descriptions as a gift from Jesus where Paul tells the believers that, "… It was he who gave some to be apostles, some to be prophets, some to be evangelists, and some to be pastors and teachers, to prepare God's people for works of service, so that the body of Christ may be built up until we all reach unity in the faith and in the knowledge of the Son of God and become mature, attaining to the whole measure of the fullness of Christ." (Ephesians 4:11-13:11).

1.4.3 Compensation and benefits

Every organization needs a salary structure for all positions. At the interview stage, when an employee emerges successful it is the duty of the human resource practitioner to finalize on the compensation and benefits. Usually the candidate would state what their expected salary package is and the human resource practitioner would indicate the offer according to the salary structure. Salary negotiations would take place and a figure arrived at. When the new staff reports, he/she is given the employment contract with the salary package and if he/she accepts the terms as indicated then he/she signs the contract and starts on the job. According to the book of Genesis, Laban negotiated for his compensation. "…Then Laban said to Jacob, 'Because you are my relative, should you therefore serve me for nothing? Tell me, what shall your wages be?'" (Genesis 29:15). In the same story, Genesis 30:28-34 states "…He continued, Name me your wages, and I will give it. But he said to him, you yourself know how I have served you and how your cattle have fared with me. '…For you had little before I came and it has increased to a multitude, and the LORD has blessed you wherever I turned. But now, when shall I provide for my own household also?'"

In my experience I have seen staff come and change, especially if they negotiated terms that have not been effected possibly because the negotiation and agreement was verbal. At the health facility, I got a lot

17

of complaints in this area. Staff made complaints on salary disharmony, that apparently salary was reviewed on favoritism. I also got complaints of staff who were requested to sign their appointment letter with a verbal promise of salary review later. In my office as a human resource practitioner, I would only act upon written instructions, if there is any salary reviews to be done then the instructions must be sent to me in writing. We see this deception illustrated in Genesis where Laban fails to give Rachel to Jacob and instead gives him Leah. We see Jacob objecting, saying these are not the terms that were agreed upon. Genesis 29:25-27 states "…So it came about in the morning that, behold, it was Leah! And he said to Laban, 'What is this you have done to me? Was it not for Rachel that I served with you? Why then have you deceived me?' But Laban said, 'It is not the practice in our place to marry off the younger before the firstborn. Complete the week of this one, and we will give you the other also for the service which you shall serve with me for another seven years.'"

I have seen a lot of protest letters of staff demanding better salary terms or threatening to quit. For positions that are hard to find, these employees would usually get a review. In such cases we always ask for the salary rate offered by our competing organizations in the industry and counter offer the rate that they have given our staff. But this does not apply in all cases, sometimes circumstances force you to let the employee go, especially if the salary demanded is beyond our means.

At the security company, we printed out small cards with employee rights and attached them together with their name tags hanging on the same lanyard. One of the employee rights listed there was a right to fair wages. The book of Numbers illustrates Moses receiving instructions to give the product of the threshing flour and wine vat as their compensation in return for their service in the tent of meeting. "You shall say to them, 'When you have offered from it the best of it, then the rest shall be reckoned to the Levites as the product of the threshing floor, and as the product of the wine vat. You may eat it anywhere, you and your households, for it is your compensation in return for your service in the tent of meeting." (Numbers 18:30-31).

The Ministry of Labor revises the wage rates from time to time. For example, in the security industry the wage rates are classified according to the cities, their job rank and the location. Hardship areas have a hardship allowance. A case in point was the revision in 2013 for basic pay from Kshs.9,572 to Kshs.10,912, and house allowance from Kshs.1,436 to Kshs.1,637 for major cities. In the parable of the workers in the vineyard in the book of Matthew, the landowner agrees with his laborers' compensation as a denarius a day and negotiates a better pay commensurate with the work done. In human resource management, we call this performance related pay. "When he had agreed with the laborers for a denarius for the day, he sent them into his vineyard... And he went out about the third hour and saw others standing idle in the market place; and to those he said, 'You also go into the vineyard, and whatever is right I will give you.' And so they went." (Matthew 20:2-4).

In every organization, the salary structure is put in different categories, such as senior management, middle-level management and frontline staff. In the security company, senior management was in category A, middle-level management in category B and frontline staff in category C. All the categories have different basic salaries and allowances. At the media company, senior management staff had a Gold medical cover, the middle-level managers had a Silver medical cover and other staff had Bronze medical cover. The higher the medical cover, the better the benefits. The book of 1Timothy gives an incident where the elders who directed the affairs of the church were said to be well worth of double honor, especially those whose work is preaching and teaching. An emphasis was given on the worker deserving his wages. "...The elders who direct the affairs of the church well are worthy of double honor, especially those whose work is preaching and teaching. For Scripture states, 'Do not muzzle an ox while it is treading out the grain, and 'The worker deserves his wages." (1Timothy 17-21).

I have seen many incidences where various employee unions organize for collective bargaining agreements where workers' wages are negotiated and agreed upon. In Kenya, usually the new wage rates are released every Labor Day, 1st May of every year. I have witnessed a number of public servants going on strike because the government has not met the agreement that was reached. A case in point is the teachers, doctors and nurses.

In December 2016, the doctors, through their union - the Kenya Medical Practitioners and Dentists Union, went on strike and up to February 2017 they were still on strike. At some point, the Court committed the union officials to a one-month jail term but they did not budge. Their bone of contention was that the Collective Bargaining Agreement signed in 2013 ought to be implemented. Their strike saw many patients lose their lives. This affected the health sector in terms of patients' influx, hospitals being full past capacity and struggle for resources, including human resources. Teachers and lecturers soon issued their strike notices and it has now become a cycle. Nurses also went on strike in June 2017 over their salary terms.

1.4.4 Employee code of conduct

This in any organization represents the organization's culture and policies. It is the organization's way of doing things. All new employees are expected to fit into the organization's culture. As Christians, the Bible gives us the principles that we are expected to practice in our day-to-day activities. The Bible gives us the norms, values and Christian practices. The book of 2 Timothy outlines the guidelines on how awards are done, that they are given to those who win according to the rules. "No one serving as a soldier gets entangled in civilian affairs, but rather tries to please his commanding officer. Similarly, anyone who competes as an athlete does not receive the victor's crown except by competing according to the rules." (2 Timothy 4:5).

Every workplace has its rules and regulations. These are usually summarized in the employee manual and made available to staff. In my experience from various industries, employee meetings have been held on a quarterly basis. In these meetings the employee manual is discussed. For example, it was a rule at the health facility that whenever a stranger or an outside salesperson came in asking for information about the hospital this person was to be directed to the Hospital Administrator's office. No staff was to give any information to a stranger. The book of Exodus illustrates some of the regulations that the Lord gave to Moses for the Passover meal. "…The LORD said to Moses and Aaron, 'these are the regulations for the Passover meal: No foreigner may eat it. Any slave you have bought may eat it after you have circumcised him, but a temporary resident or a hired worker may not eat it. It must be eaten inside the house; take none of the meat outside the house. Do not break any of the bones. The whole community of Israel must celebrate it. 'A foreigner residing among you who wants to celebrate the LORD's Passover must have all the males in his household circumcised; then he may take part like one born in the land. No uncircumcised male may eat it. The same law applies both to the native-born and to the foreigner residing among you."(Exodus 12:43-48).

At the security company, the employee code of conduct was referred to as the Business Ethics Policy. This was developed around a core set of values which are fundamental to the organization's development and success. The book of Exodus give us God's commandments. "…And God spoke all these words: 'I am the LORD your God, who brought you out of Egypt, out of the land of slavery. You shall have no other gods before me. You shall not make for yourself an image in the form of anything in heaven above or on the earth beneath or in the waters below. You shall not bow down to them or worship them; for I, the LORD your God, am a jealous God, punishing the children for the sin of the parents to the third and fourth generation of those who hate me, but showing love to a thousand generations of those who love me and keep my commandments. You shall not misuse the name of the LORD your God, for the LORD will not hold anyone guiltless who misuses his name. Remember the Sabbath day by keeping it holy. Six days you shall labor and do all your work, but the seventh day is a Sabbath to the LORD your God. On it you shall not do any work, neither you, nor your son or daughter, nor your male or female servant, nor your animals, nor any foreigner residing in your towns. For in six days the LORD made the heavens and the earth, the sea, and all that is in them, but he rested on the seventh day. Therefore the LORD blessed the Sabbath day and made it holy. Honor your father and your mother, so that you may live long in the land the LORD your God is giving you. "You shall not murder. You shall not commit adultery. You shall not steal. You shall not give false testimony against your neighbor. You shall not covet your neighbor's house. You shall not covet your neighbor's wife, or his male or female servant, his ox or donkey, or anything that belongs to your neighbor."(Exodus 20:1-17). The book of Deuteronomy 5:1-22 also gives the Lord's commandments.

All employers are called upon to ensure equal treatment for all staff. The books of James and Peter give us an example where Christians are warned against discrimination between the rich and the poor. "My brothers and sisters, believers in our glorious Lord Jesus Christ must not show favoritism. Suppose a man comes into your meeting wearing a gold ring and fine clothes, and a poor man in filthy old clothes also comes in. If you show special attention to the man wearing fine clothes and say, 'Here's a good seat for you,' but say to the poor man, 'You stand there' or 'Sit on the floor by my feet, have you not discriminated among yourselves and become judges with evil thoughts? But if you show favoritism, you sin and are convicted by the law as lawbreakers." (James 2:1-4) and 1 Peter 1:17 states "…Since you call on a Father who judges each person's work impartially…"

Employees are expected to obey their employers' instructions. The book of Colossians illustrate that wives are supposed to submit to their husbands; husbands to love their wives; children to obey their parents; parents to be good role models to their children; and workers to obey their employers. "Wives, submit yourselves to your husbands, as is fitting in the Lord… Husbands, love your wives and do not be harsh with them. Children, obey your parents in everything, for this pleases the Lord. Fathers, do not embitter your children, or they will become discouraged. Slaves obey your earthly masters in everything; and do it, not only when their eye is on you and to curry their favor, but with sincerity of heart and reverence for the Lord. Whatever you do, work at it with all your heart, as working for the Lord, not for human masters, since you know that you will receive an inheritance from the Lord as a reward. It is the Lord Christ you are serving. Anyone who does wrong will be repaid for their wrongs, and there is no favoritism." (Colossians 3:18-25); and the letter to Colossians 4:1 states "Masters, provide your slaves with what is right and fair, because you know that you also have a Master in heaven."

The books of Romans, 1Timothy and Titus illustrate that everyone is called upon to subject to the governing authorities, for there is no authority except that which God has established. "Let everyone be subject to the governing authorities, for there is no authority except that which God has established. The authorities that exist have been established by God. Consequently, whoever rebels against the authority is rebelling against what God has instituted, and those who do so will bring judgment on themselves… For rulers hold no terror for those who do right, but for those who do wrong. Do you want to be free from fear of the one in authority? Then do what is right and you will be commended. For the one in authority is God's servant for your good. But if you do wrong, be afraid, for rulers do not bear the sword for no reason. They are God's servants, agents of wrath to bring punishment on the wrongdoer. Therefore, it is necessary to submit to the authorities, not only because of possible punishment but also as a matter of conscience. This is also why you pay taxes, for the authorities are God's servants, who give their full time to governing. Give to everyone what you owe them: If you owe taxes, pay taxes; if revenue, then revenue; if respect, then respect; if honor, then honor." (Romans 13: 1-7).

I have handled very many cases of insubordination in all the industries I have worked in. The Employment Act 2007 Section 44 states the grounds for lawful dismissal. "...an employee knowingly fails, or refuses, to obey a lawful and proper command which it was within the scope of his duty to obey, issued by his employer or a person placed in authority over him by his employer..." 1 Timothy 6:1-2 states "All who are under the yoke of slavery should consider their masters worthy of full respect, so that God's name and our teaching may not be slandered. Those who have believing masters should not show them disrespect just because they are fellow believers. Instead, they should serve them even better because their masters are dear to them as fellow believers and are devoted to the welfare of their slaves." The book of Titus relates to the same code of conduct. "...Remind the people to be subject to rulers and authorities, to be obedient, to be ready to do whatever is good, to slander no one, to be peaceable and considerate, and always to be gentle toward everyone." (Titus 3:1-2).

Colossians 3:22 states "...Slaves, obey in everything those who are your earthly masters, not by way of eye-service, as people-pleasers, but with sincerity of heart, fearing the Lord." In the same code of conduct, the book of Ephesians 6:1-9 states, "Children, obey your parents in the Lord, for this is right. Honor your father and mother—which is the first commandment with a promise—so that it may go well with you and that you may enjoy long life on the earth. Fathers, do not exasperate your children; instead, bring them up in the training and instruction of the Lord. Slaves, obey your earthly masters with respect and fear, and with sincerity of heart, just as you would obey Christ. Obey them not only to win their favor when their eye is on you, but as slaves of Christ, doing the will of God from your heart. Serve wholeheartedly, as if you were serving the Lord, not people, because you know that the Lord will reward each one for whatever good they do, whether they are slave or free. And masters, treat your slaves in the same way. Do not threaten them, since you know that he who is both their Master and yours is in heaven, and there is no favoritism with him."

At the security company, the core values included best people, integrity, customer focus, teamwork and collaboration, and performance. The book of 1Peter outlines some of these core values. "…Be shepherds of God's flock that is under your care, watching over them—not because you must, but because you are willing, as God wants you to be; not pursuing dishonest gain, but eager to serve; not lording it over those entrusted to you, but being examples to the flock. And when the Chief Shepherd appears, you will receive the crown of glory that will never fade away. In the same way, you who are younger, submit yourselves to your elders. All of you, clothe yourselves with humility toward one another, because, God opposes the proud but shows favor to the humble. Humble yourselves, therefore, under God's mighty hand, that he may lift you up in due time. Cast all your anxiety on him because he cares for you." (1Peter 5:2-6)

At the security company, we recognized staff who had upheld or lived the core values of the company and awarded them so as to encourage the other staff to emulate their example. For example, a security guard manning an ATM saw a client withdraw money and drop some of the money on the floor; the security guard with high integrity called the client back and gave them the money. This staff received a good review from the client and subsequently, an award from the company.

At the health facility, the core values included honesty and integrity, teamwork, respect and fairness, professionalism, among others. The Gospel of Luke gives a guideline to Christians to treat others as they would wish to be treated. In a workplace employees are required to treat each other with respect and fairness. "…And as you wish that others would do to you, do so to them." (Luke 6:31)

Everyone is called upon to pay taxes and debts owed. Additionally, they are called upon to respect and honor those in authority. Disrespect is a disciplinary offence in the human resource practice. Every employed person in Kenya earning a gross salary of Kshs.10,000 and above is supposed to pay tax (Pay As You Earn). Additionally, in the day-to-day operations, a staff may damage the organization's property and be asked to pay. In my practice, I have asked staff to pay for damaged property, lost monies or payment of monies in lieu of notice upon resignation. The challenge comes when staffs wait until they receive their salaries before they disappear or hand in their resignation.

The core value of love for one another is outlined in the Gospel of Luke in an incident where a lawyer asks Jesus what he must do to inherit eternal life. Jesus responds by saying that the requirement is to love the Lord God with all his heart and with all his soul and with all his strength and with his entire mind, and his neighbor as himself. "And behold, a lawyer stood up to put him to the test, saying, "Teacher, what shall I do to inherit eternal life?" He said to him, "What is written in the Law? How do you read it?" And he answered, "You shall love the Lord your God with all your heart and with all your soul and with all your strength and with all your mind, and your neighbor as yourself." And he said to him, "You have answered correctly; do this, and you will live."(Luke 10:25-28).

In my experience across the industries we have always had a culture of greeting one another, celebrating occasions together and mourning with our fellow colleagues in cases of bereavement. While in college I was taught that just as a teacher ought to know his/her student by name, so should a human resource practitioner. I have been both a teacher and a human resource practitioner. Sometimes staff would walk in my office and be surprised that I know them by their full names. In the health facility, we always had morning assemblies where all staff would meet, regardless of their religion, pray together and share their experiences. We have always shown unity and love for one another. We celebrated birthdays for staff from January to December of each year.

According to the Gospel of Matthew, Mark and the book of Proverbs, Christians ought to forgive one another. "...For if you forgive others their trespasses, your heavenly Father will also forgive you, but if you do not forgive others their trespasses, neither will your Father forgive your trespasses." (Matthew 6:14-15). Matthew 18: 21-35 states, "...Then Peter came up and said to him, 'Lord, how often will my brother sin against me, and I forgive him? As many as seven times? Jesus said to him, 'I do not say to you seven times, but seventy times seven. Therefore the kingdom of heaven may be compared to a king who wished to settle accounts with his servants. When he began to settle, one was brought to him who owed him ten thousand talents. And since he could not pay, his master ordered him to be sold, with his wife and children and all that he had, and payment to be made.'" The book of Proverbs shows Christians being advised against revenge. "...Do not say, 'I will do to him as he has done to me; I will pay the man back for what he has done.'" (Proverbs 24:29)

In any work situation, employees are likely to commit disciplinary offences, for example lateness, absence from work, among others. Such offences may warrant a cautionary letter, a verbal warning before written warnings apply. In such cases, the employee is forgiven and given another chance to prove themselves. While at the media company, there was a manager who always reported to work late. He would even come to the office dressed in jeans and would not care. This manager was reporting to the chief executive officer. One day the chief executive officer tasked my department to print out the biometric data for this manager for one month. The data did not give good results. This manager was then warned that should this trend be noted again, he would receive the appropriate disciplinary action.

In the health facility I mediated in a grievance case between two staff who had been friends for a long time. One of the staff would crack funny jokes regarding her friend's work. This friend never thought of it as offensive until one day the joke bordered a line which would imply incompetence. Her reaction was to call her estranged friend in her mother tongue and seriously insult her. On a Monday morning, the victim came to my office with the recording of the abusive conversation. Once I established that they were friends and the friendship had gone sour, I asked them to apologize to one another; forgive one another and go back to work.

The Gospel of Mark and the letter of Paul to the Ephesians highlight some of the wrongdoings from within and out of the heart of man, evil thoughts, sexual immorality, theft, murder, adultery, coveting, wickedness, deceit, sensuality, envy, slander, pride, foolishness."...And he said, "What comes out of a person is what defiles him. For from within, out of the heart of man, come evil thoughts, sexual immorality, theft, murder, adultery, coveting, wickedness, deceit, sensuality, envy, slander, pride, foolishness." (Mark 7:20-22).

Some of these wrongdoings are considered as disciplinary offences in workplaces. I have handled a number of disciplinary hearings on cases of fraud, theft, dishonesty, use of abusive language, among others. I have seen cases of fraud almost monthly in all workplaces I have been. I have also received complaints from staff having been abused, sexually harassed or mocked. "...Let the thief no longer steal, but rather let him labor, doing honest work with his own hands, so that he may have something to share with anyone in need." (Ephesians 4:28).

At the security company, integrity was one of the core values. Integrity means that you can always be trusted to do the right thing. One of the senior managers was fired on grounds of questionable integrity. He went against the anti-bribery policy and put the image of the company in jeopardy. The book of Isaiah 33:15-16 states, "…He who walks righteously and speaks uprightly, who despises the gain of oppressions, who shakes his hands, lest they hold a bribe, who stops his ears from hearing of bloodshed and shuts his eyes from looking on evil, he will dwell on the heights; his place of defense will be the fortresses of rocks; his bread will be given him; his water will be sure."

An employee code of conduct therefore gives the rules and regulations of any workplace. We see two incidents in Deuteronomy and Leviticus where Moses gives the Israelites guidance on how they should carry themselves around with regard to God's commandments. He tells them to listen to the statutes and the rules that he was teaching them, and to do them, that they may live. They were to go in and take possession of the land that the Lord, the God of their fathers, is giving them. They were not to add anything to the word that he commanded them, nor take from it, that they may keep the commandments of the Lord their God. "…And now, O Israel, listen to the statutes and the rules that I am teaching you, and do them, that you may live, and go in and take possession of the land that the Lord, the God of your fathers, is giving you. You shall not add to the word that I command you, nor take from it, that you may keep the commandments of the Lord your God that I command you. Your eyes have seen what the Lord did at Baal-peor, for the Lord your God destroyed from among you all the men who followed the Baal of Peor. But you who held fast to the Lord your God are all alive today. See, I have taught you statutes and rules, as the Lord my God commanded me that you should do them in the land that you are entering to take possession of it . . ." (Deuteronomy 4:1-49)

The book of Leviticus gives an example of God's reward to the Israelites if they are to observe the commandments. "You shall not make idols for yourselves or erect an image or pillar, and you shall not set up a figured stone in your land to bow down to it, for I am the Lord your God. You shall keep my Sabbaths and reverence my sanctuary: I am the Lord. "If you walk in my statutes and observe my commandments and do them, then I will give you your rains in their season, and the land shall yield its increase, and the trees of the field shall yield their fruit. Your threshing shall last to the time of the grape harvest, and the grape harvest shall last to the time for sowing. And you shall eat your bread to the full and dwell in your land securely . . ." (Leviticus 26:1-46).

The book of 2 Timothy illustrates the importance of having an employee code of conduct in place. "…All Scripture is breathed out by God and profitable for teaching, for reproof, for correction, and for training in righteousness, that the man of God may be competent, equipped for every good work." (2 Timothy 3:16-17). Human resource practitioners should inform staff that the purpose of the employee code of conduct is not punitive but rather to keep everyone in check.

In the health facility, one employee came to me and narrated her story. She was once a house help, a stripper in the night clubs, she performed odd jobs just to make ends meet. She was a single mother of three children and was the sole bread winner. At some point, her first born, a boy, became a teenager and she had to stop stripping in clubs in fear that she could meet her son in such a place. Such an employee may be judged by others or even mocked. This however, as indicated in the Gospel of Matthew, is passing judgment. "Judge not, that you be not judged. For with the judgment you pronounce you will be judged, and with the measure you use it will be measured to you. Why do you see the speck that is in your brother's eye, but do not notice the log that is in your own eye? Or how can you say to your brother, 'Let me take the speck out of your eye,' when there is the log in your own eye? You hypocrite, first take the log out of your own eye, and then you will see clearly to take the speck out of your brother's eye."(Matthew 7:1-5). In any workplace it is the work of the human resource practitioner to see to it that all employees are treated fairly. I have formulated a harassment and bullying policy in the places I have worked in order to curb such cases.

2.0 TRAINING AND DEVELOPMENT

There are various forms of training categorized into on-the-job training and off-the-job training. Training is very important, ranging from increasing an organization's productivity to motivating employees. All training requires planning; from identifying training needs, to designing a training program, finding a training facilitator, selecting training participants, content, a venue, organizing for training materials and meals. All this must be included in the training budget. The Bible gives us some examples where people were trained so as to better perform their duties.

While working in the media company, I organized a training for middle-level managers on supervisory skills. I sourced for a training facilitator, a venue, meals, training materials and worked with the facilitator to design the training program. The book of Daniel gives us an example where the king gave instructions on a training plan. "… Then the king commanded Ashpenaz, his chief eunuch, to bring some of the people of Israel, both of the royal family and of the nobility, youths without blemish, of good appearance and skillful in all wisdom, endowed with knowledge, understanding learning, and competent to stand in the king's palace, and to teach them the literature and language of the Chaldeans. The king assigned them a daily portion of the food that the king ate, and of the wine that he drank. They were to be educated for three years, and at the end of that time they were to stand before the king. Among these were Daniel, Hananiah, Mishael, and Azariah of the tribe of Judah. And the chief of the eunuchs gave them names: Daniel he called Belteshazzar, Hananiah he called Shadrach,

Mishael he called Meshach, and Azariah he called Abednego . . ." (Daniel 1:3-21).

In the security company, I organized a lot of trainings for security officers. Basically, after every recruitment, we would conduct two weeks' trainings before placing the security officers at their duty stations. The book of 1 Samuel gives an example of training application. After training, the participants are expected to apply the skills that they have acquired in their day-to-day work activities. "...And David said to his men, 'Every man strap on his sword!' And every man of them strapped on his sword. David also strapped on his sword. And about four hundred men went up after David, while two hundred remained with the baggage." (1 Samuel 25:13).

At the health facility, we organized different trainings for different departments. For example, the pharmacy staffs were trained on stock management and drug supply chain. This training would not be beneficial to a cashier. We also organized training for cashiers on a new system that would affect how to charge for medical services offered to a special category of patients brought in through a service level contract with a charity organization. The cashiers' training would not be relevant to a staff in pharmacy.

At the media company, we organized for a talent search in various universities around Nairobi to identify students who had potential to be radio presenters. One of the criteria we used was that the students must be in their final year of study and aged 18 and above. The successful students would then be brought on board as presenter trainees. The book of Numbers gives us similar examples where Moses and Aaron are asked to list the Israelites from 20 years old upward, that were able to go to war. These men aged 20 and above had undergone prior training on fighting. "...From twenty years old and upward, all in Israel who are able to go to war, you and Aaron shall list them, company by company." (Numbers 1:3).

It is important that a human resource practitioner ensures that the staffs are competent and equipped for the duties they are to perform. This is the reason why a training-needs analysis is done. Through the training-needs analysis, one is able to identify the training gaps and organize for training to close the gaps. At the health facility, a new machine was bought for the radiology department and the staffs in this department were trained on the use of this equipment. The book of 2

Timothy outlines the importance of training. "...That the man of God may be competent, equipped for every good work." (2 Timothy 3:17).

The main goal for training at any workplace is to ensure that you have competent and well equipped staff. The Occupational Health and Safety Act 2007, Section 6 indicates that it is the duty of the employer to ensure the employees are trained and well equipped for the job that they are to do. One of the challenges I have encountered is inadequate supply of equipment by the top-level management. Employees are therefore forced to improvise, leading to work injuries or low quality results. The ripple effect therefore becomes implementation of the Work Injury and Benefits Act 2007 where you have to compensate staff for the injuries both permanent and temporary.

At the manufacturing company, every morning an alarm would be sounded and all staff assembled at a square, held hands and recited the Kaizen philosophy. This philosophy is a tool to improve quality, productivity, safety and workplace culture. According to the Gospel of Matthew, Jesus taught his disciples how to pray. "...Pray then like this: 'Our Father in heaven, hallowed be your name. Your kingdom come, your will be done, on earth as it is in heaven. Give us this day our daily bread, and forgive us our debts, as we also have forgiven our debtors. And lead us not into temptation, but deliver us from evil." (Matthew 6:9-13).

Training increases an employee's knowledge. At the health facility, we had a continuous medical training every Wednesday. In these trainings, staff would gain new knowledge on the developments in the field of medicine. According to the Gospel of Luke, Jesus is said to have increased in wisdom and in stature and in favor with God and man. "... And Jesus increased in wisdom and in stature and in favor with God and man." (Luke 2:52).

There was a challenge at the health facility with customer service. Despite the fact that all staff were trained on excellent customer service skills, we would still receive complaints on rude or unfriendly staff. We kept reminding staff to practice what they had learnt in the training. The first week after training everyone was on their "A-game" on customer service, only to lose the psyche after a month or so. The book of 2 Timothy gives us an example where Timothy is advised to continue practicing what he had learnt. ". . . But as for you, continue in what you have learned and have firmly believed, knowing from whom you learned it." (2 Timothy 3:14).

Refresher courses are always advisable to remind the staff what they had learnt initially. While at the security company, we organized refresher courses for drivers on defensive driving every year. The book of Hebrews gives us an example of this when Paul tells the believers that they needed someone to teach them again the basic principles of the oracles of God. "...About this we have much to say, and it is hard to explain, since you have become dull of hearing. For though by this time you ought to be teachers, you need someone to teach you again the basic principles of the oracles of God. You need milk, not solid food, for everyone who lives on milk is unskilled in the word of righteousness, since he is a child. But solid food is for the mature, for those who have their powers of discernment trained by constant practice to distinguish good from evil." (Hebrews 5:11-14).

It is important for employees to appreciate the investment that an employer puts in them through training. At the media company, we were giving graduate trainees a training agreement bond for three years to fresh graduates from school. The main reason for this was to get return on investment. Such employees, at their end of the training bond, would write very good reviews, thanking management for investing in them. The book of Psalms gives an example of David showing gratitude to God. "...Of David. Blessed be the Lord, my rock, who trains my hands for war, and my fingers for battle" (Psalm 144:1).

When a new staff reports to work on the first day, the other employees are encouraged to teach them how to do things. It is not just the responsibility of the head of department; all staffs are expected to demonstrate team work. At the health facility, I had an incident where a trainee in the laboratory department went to bleed a client and did it the wrong way. This trainee was supposed to be under supervision at all times. As a result of having no one to watch over him at the time of bleeding, the client wrote a message complaining about the quality of services at the facility. According to the Gospel of Matthew, we all ought to teach others on God's commandments. "...Therefore whoever relaxes one of the least of these commandments and teaches others to do the same will be called least in the kingdom of heaven, but whoever does them and teaches them will be called great in the kingdom of heaven." (Matthew 5:19).

In any facility we have staff we call seasoned employees, those who have served an organization for over 10 years. At the security company, we had disciplinary cases mostly with young staff and those who had served under two years in the organization. The seasoned employees would make comments such as, "These young fellows have no idea how far we have come as a company." They would then encourage the new staff and share their experiences. The book of Proverbs gives an illustration of how sons ought to hear their fathers' instructions, and be attentive, that they may gain insight, and are asked not to forsake this teaching. "Hear, O sons, a father's instruction, and be attentive, that you may gain insight, for I give you good precepts; do not forsake my teaching. When I was a son with my father, tender, the only one in the sight of my mother, he taught me and said to me, "Let your heart hold fast my words; keep my commandments, and live. Get wisdom; get insight; do not forget, and do not turn away from the words of my mouth." (Proverbs 4:1-13).

It is possible to make reference to the lessons from a training to explain a point. While working at the security company, we informed all drivers that it is their responsibility to ensure that they have done the vehicle checklist every morning, checking that the vehicle is in good condition to drive. One day a driver refused to go on duty with the company car because it was not fit to be on the road as per the vehicle checklist. The manager reported the case to me as a disciplinary matter but since the Occupational Health and Safety Act 2007 states that an employee should not be punished for refusing to perform a task that jeopardizes his/her safety, I advised the manager to ensure the vehicle is fixed or to approve in writing for the vehicle to go on the road as it is and take liability. According to the Occupational Health and Safety Act 2007, Section 8, "An occupier shall not dismiss an employee, injure the employee or discriminate against or disadvantage an employee in respect of the employee's employment, or alter the employee's position to the detriment of the employee by reason only that the employee —— (a) makes a complaint about a matter which the employee considers is not safe or is a risk to his health;(b) is a member of a safety and health committee established pursuant to this Act; or(c) exercises any of his functions as a member of the safety and health committee."

According to the Gospel of Matthew, Jesus told the devil that it was written that man shall not live by bread alone, but by every word that comes from the mouth of God. Jesus quoted the Bible. Once an employee has been trained, he/she can refer to the content that he/she was taught and use it somewhere else relevant. "Then Jesus was led up by the Spirit into the wilderness to be tempted by the devil. And after fasting forty days and forty nights, he was hungry. And the tempter came and said to him, "If you are the Son of God, command these stones to become loaves of bread." But he answered, "It is written, 'Man shall not live by bread alone, but by every word that comes from the mouth of God.' Then the devil took him to the holy city and set him on the pinnacle of the temple."(Matthew 4:1-25).

In my role as a human resource practitioner, I have always held quarterly meetings with my staff to take them through the staff manual and to sensitize them on new developments, for example, on their medical cover, pension scheme administration, leave status, among other things. The Gospel of Matthew gives us an instance where Jesus goes up on the mountain, sits down with his disciples and teaches them about the poor, the bereaved, the meek and the subsequent blessings that these people will receive. "Seeing the crowds, he went up on the mountain, and when he sat down, his disciples came to him. And he opened his mouth and taught them, saying: "Blessed are the poor in spirit, for theirs is the kingdom of heaven. "Blessed are those who mourn, for they shall be comforted. "Blessed are the meek, for they shall inherit the earth." (Matthew 5:1-48).

The book of 2 Chronicles illustrates the importance of training application. The Lord blessed Jehoshaphat because he walked in the earlier ways of his father David. He did not seek the Baals, but sought the God of his father and walked in his commandments, and not according to the practices of Israel. Once a staff is trained, they are to be evaluated to see if they are applying the training they underwent. Jehoshaphat applied the teaching he learnt from David. "…Jehoshaphat his son reigned in his place and strengthened himself against Israel. He placed forces in all the fortified cities of Judah and set garrisons in the land of Judah, and in the cities of Ephraim that Asa his father had captured. The Lord was with Jehoshaphat, because he walked in the earlier ways of his father David. He did not seek the Baals, but sought the God of his father and walked in his commandments, and not according to the practices of Israel. Therefore the Lord established the kingdom in his hand. And all Judah brought tribute to Jehoshaphat, and he had great riches and honor." (2 Chronicles 17:1-19).

When we were conducting the ISO certification process at the health facility, we had to develop standard operating procedures for all departments. These standard operating procedures were to be adhered to in the day-to-day running of operations in the facility. Paul alludes to the same in the book of Romans when he says whatever was written in former days; was written for their instruction, that through endurance and through the encouragement of the Scriptures they might have hope. "...For whatever was written in former days was written for our instruction, that through endurance and through the encouragement of the Scriptures we might have hope." (Romans 15:4). In the ISO certification process at the health facility, some employees were trained to become internal auditors of the entire ISO process. They underwent a training and thereafter, an evaluation and certification as auditors. According to the Gospel of Matthew, Jesus commissioned the disciples to go and make disciples of all nations, baptizing them in the name of the Father and of the Son and of the Holy Spirit. "Go therefore and make disciples of all nations, baptizing them in the name of the Father and of the Son and of the Holy Spirit." (Matthew 28:19).

A trainer uses real life examples to illustrate a point. The Gospel of Luke shows Jesus using a parable to teach the disciples about concern for others. "...Jesus replied, 'A man was going down from Jerusalem to Jericho, and he fell among robbers, who stripped him and beat him and departed, leaving him half dead. Now by chance a priest was going down that road, and when he saw him he passed by on the other side. So likewise a Levite, when he came to the place and saw him, passed by on the other side. But a Samaritan, as he journeyed, came to where he was, and when he saw him, he had compassion. He went to him and bound up his wounds, pouring on oil and wine. Then he set him on his own animal and brought him to an inn and took care of him . . ." (Luke 10:30-37). Additionally, the book of Proverbs gives an instance where parents are told to train their children in the way they should go and assurance is given that they will learn and adhere to it. "...Train up a child in the way he should go; even when he is old he will not depart from it." (Proverbs 22:6).

3.0 PERFORMANCE MANAGEMENT

Performance management is a much broader and complicated function of human resource management, as it encompasses activities such as joint goal setting, continuous progress review and frequent communication, feedback and coaching for improved performance, implementation of employee development programs and rewarding achievements. This is usually done based on the key performance indicators linked to the overall organization's strategic plan. Employees will usually be assessed based on how each one of them has performed in relation to the key performance indicators. The process helps in identifying training gaps in employees, identifying staffs who are non-performers, seeing the organization's performance, motivating staff, among other reasons.

When a new employee reports, among the first documents that he/she receives are his/her performance targets. These are targets against which employees are assessed in the performance appraisal process. In the health facility, I always ensured performance targets for all staff are set by the first three months of the year. These targets are done in two copies such that one is given to the staff and the other is kept in their personal files. When the staffs sign their performance targets I tell that that as they go about performing their duties, they should know that their work will be gauged based on the targets set. The book of 1 Corinthians gives an example where Paul tells the believers that whatever they do should be to the glory of God. "...so, whether you eat or drink, or whatever you do, do all to the glory of God." (1 Corinthians 10:31) This, in human resource management, would be like individual evaluation during a performance appraisal process.

The performance appraisal process is in three steps. The first step is the self-appraisal or individual evaluation. Here the employee introspectively evaluates his/her performance against set performance targets. Employees are required to prepare for their performance appraisals and book an appraisal interview with the supervisor/evaluator at least one week before the due date. Further, support documentation may be required to avoid a rebuttal or subjectivity as performance evaluation should be based on fact. According to the book of Galatians, Paul told the Christians to each test his/her own work, and then his/her reason to boast will be in him/her alone and not in his/her neighbor. "…For if anyone thinks he is something, when he is nothing, he deceives himself. But let each one test his own work, and then his reason to boast will be in him alone and not in his neighbor." (Galatians 6:3-4).

According to the book of 2 Corinthians, Paul asked the believers to examine themselves to see whether they are in the faith. "…Examine yourselves to see whether you are in the faith; test yourselves. Do you not realize that Christ Jesus is in you—unless, of course, you fail the test? And I trust that you will discover that we have not failed the test." (2 Corinthians 13:5-6). In a workplace you would find midyear appraisals and end of year appraisals. Employees are evaluated and shown their areas of weaknesses in the midyear appraisal and the same is reviewed at the end of year appraisal. The book of 1 Thessalonians 5:21 states, "…But test everything; hold fast what is good." All employees should aim at enhancing the organization's productivity through excellent performance. The book of Colossians gives an instance where Paul advises the Colossians that whatever they do, they should do it with all their heart. "…whatever you do, work at it with all your heart, as working for the Lord, not for human masters." (Colossians 3:23).

Professionalism was one of the core values at the health facility. All employees were expected to uphold this core value. There was a complaint from a client regarding a staff who was too quick to finish with a patient that he forgot to finish the process of discharging the patient properly. According to the book of 2 Corinthians, Paul told the believers to finish doing the work they desired so that their readiness in desiring it may be matched by their completing it out of what they had. "…And in this matter I give my judgment: this benefits you, who a year ago started not only to do this work but also to desire to do it. So now finish doing it as well, so that your readiness in desiring it may be matched by your completing it out of what you have." (2 Corinthians 8:10-11).

At the sermon on the mountain, Jesus tells the crowds to let their light shine before others so that they may see their good works and give glory to their Father who is in heaven. "…In the same way, let your light shine before others, so that they may see your good works and give glory to your Father who is in heaven." (Matthew 5:16). At the security company, performance was one of the core values of the organization. Each regional manager had the sales targets and debt collection targets that were to be met at the end of every month. The Service Delivery Manager for Western Region was promoted to the position of Regional Service Delivery Manager, covering a bigger region than the previous one because of his excellent performance.

Paul informs the Philippians of the performance target that he has set for himself and what he must do to accomplish it. He says that he does not consider himself yet to have taken hold of it. But one thing he would do was to forget what is behind and strain toward what is ahead. He would press on toward the goal to win the prize for which God has called him heavenward in Christ Jesus. "…Brothers and sisters, I do not consider myself yet to have taken hold of it. But one thing I do: Forgetting what is behind and straining toward what is ahead, I press on toward the goal to win the prize for which God has called me heavenward in Christ Jesus." (Philippians 3:13-14).

At the health facility, there was a head of department who was proceeding for study leave and needed to have somebody take over her duties in an acting capacity. The person that the head of department had chosen stood her ground that she would not be able to perform the tasks ahead of her. We then had to sit down with her and look at the challenges that she was foreseeing and guide her through how she would handle the challenges. Eventually she took on the role. The book of Numbers gives an example of some men going to Caleb and saying that they were not able to go up against the people, for they are stronger than they were. "…Then the men who had gone up with him said, 'We are not able to go up against the people, for they are stronger than we are." (Numbers 13:31).

The book of Romans outlines the importance of a performance management system. Paul highlights the benefits of good performance and the consequences of poor performance. He says God will repay each person according to what they have done. Those who by persistence in doing good seek glory, honor and immortality will receive eternal life. But for those who are self-seeking and who reject the truth and follow evil, there will be wrath and anger. There will be trouble and distress for every human being who does evil. "God will repay each person according to what they have done. To those who by persistence in doing good seek glory, honor and immortality, he will give eternal life. But for those who are self-seeking and who reject the truth and follow evil, there will be wrath and anger. There will be trouble and distress for every human being who does evil: first for the Jew, then for the Gentile; but glory, honor and peace for everyone who does good: first for the Jew, then for the Gentile. For God does not show favoritism." (Romans 2:6-11).

At the beginning of every year almost all organizations review employees' salaries. Some of the reviews are usually a flat rate across the board but others consider the performance of the employee and allocate a percentage of a salary increment based on the appraisal score. The Gospel of Matthew gives us an example of a man going on a journey calling his servants and entrusting to them his property. To one he gave five talents, to another two, to another one, to each according to his ability. Then he went away. He who had received the five talents went at once and traded with them, and he made five talents more. Also he who had the two talents made two talents more. But he who had received one talent went and dug in the ground and hid his master's money. "For it will be like a man going on a journey, who called his servants and entrusted to them his property. To one he gave five talents, to another two, to another one, to each according to his ability. Then he went away. He who had received the five talents went at once and traded with them, and he made five talents more. So also he who had the two talents made two talents more. But he who had received the one talent went and dug in the ground and hid his master's money." (Matthew 25:14-28). This is to indicate performance related pay. The master rewarded the first two according to how much they had made and the one who did not invest the talents loses what he had to the two servants who had invested what they had been given.

Performance related pay is also outlined in the book of Genesis in the story of Adam and the Garden of Eden. "...And to Adam he said, 'Because you have listened to the voice of your wife and have eaten of the tree of which I commanded you, 'You shall not eat of it,' cursed is the ground because of you; in pain you shall eat of it all the days of your life; thorns and thistles it shall bring forth for you; and you shall eat the plants of the field. By the sweat of your face you shall eat bread, till you return to the ground, for out of it you were taken; for you are dust, and to dust you shall return." (Genesis 3:17-19).

The book of Hosea illustrates an example where Jacob took on work to get a wife. This is a performance related pay; where he took care of the sheep and in return he was to get a wife. "…Now Jacob fled to the land of Aram, And Israel worked for a wife, And for a wife he kept sheep." (Hosea 12:12).

4.0 REWARD AND COMPENSATION

Reward and compensation is about paying staff for the work they have done for you. This might be in the form of salaries, wages, benefits, goods and services. The book of 1 Corinthians gives an illustration of a person planting a vineyard and eating its grapes. ". . Who serves as a soldier at his own expense? Who plants a vineyard and does not eat its grapes? Who tends a flock and does not drink the milk? Do I say this merely on human authority? Doesn't the Law say the same thing? For it is written in the Law of Moses: "Do not muzzle an ox while it is treading out the grain." Is it about oxen that God is concerned? Surely he says this for us, doesn't he? Yes, this was written for us, because whoever plows and threshes should be able to do so in the hope of sharing in the harvest. If we have sown spiritual seed among you, is it too much if we reap a material harvest from you? If others have this right of support from you, shouldn't we have it all the more?" (1Corinthians 9:7,11).

The book of Corinthians goes further to illustrate that preachers should earn their living by the gospel. "...If we have sown spiritual things among you, is it too much if we reap material things from you?" (1 Corinthians 9:11) and 1 Corinthians 9:14 states, ". . . In the same way, the Lord commanded that those who proclaim the gospel should get their living by the gospel." Reward and compensation is usually predetermined based on the organization's performance; the type of work; terms of services; academic qualifications; and experience, among others. The book of Romans 4:4 states, "...Now to him that worketh is the reward not reckoned of grace, but of debt."

In Genesis 29:15, Genesis 30:28-36, we see Laban and Jacob negotiating for Jacob's reward. Laban asks Jacob to name his wages, and Jacob in return says he would work for seven years in return for Laban's younger daughter, Rachel.

According to the book of 2 Kings, the priests at the entrance of the temple paid the carpenters and builders, the masons and stonecutters who worked on the temple of the LORD. "When the amount had been determined, they gave the money to the men appointed to supervise the work on the temple. With it they paid those who worked on the temple of the LORD—the carpenters and builders, the masons and stonecutters. They purchased timber and blocks of dressed stone for the repair of the temple of the LORD, and met all the other expenses of restoring the temple. The money brought into the temple was not spent for making silver basins, wick trimmers, sprinkling bowls, trumpets or any other articles of gold or silver for the temple of the LORD; it was paid to the workers, who used it to repair the temple. They did not require an accounting from those to whom they gave the money to pay the workers, because they acted with complete honesty." (2 Kings 12:11). This is to show that all workers are supposed to be paid for the work they have done.

Chapter 22 of the same book shows King Josiah asking the high priest to get ready the money that had been brought into God's temple and entrust it to the men appointed to supervise the work on the temple. These men would in turn pay the workers who repair the temple of the LORD. "…Go up to Hilkiah the high priest and have him get ready the money that has been brought into the temple of the LORD, which the doorkeepers have collected from the people. Have them entrust it to the men appointed to supervise the work on the temple. And have these men pay the workers who repair the temple of the LORD—the carpenters, the builders and the masons. Also have them purchase timber and dressed stone to repair the temple. But they need not account for the money entrusted to them, because they are honest in their dealings." (2 Kings 22:2-7).

I have had an opportunity to work with different types of employees; casual employees, term contracts and permanent and pensionable employees. All these types of employees have different payment terms and modes of payments. The casual staffs are paid their wages at a daily rate, the term contracts and permanent staff would be paid at the end of the month in arrears. The amount of salary to be paid would depend on the type of job and the entry level salary for the particular job. At the media company; salaries for employees were paid by the 28th of every month. The deadline for payroll instructions was the 15th of every month. We would send instructions on new employees, or any new changes in an employee's salary. The book of Ezra gives an example where stonemasons and the carpenters were paid for the services they had rendered. "The people gave money to pay stonemasons and the carpenters…" (Ezra 3:7).

According to the book of 2 Kings the priests paid the carpenters and the builders who worked on the house of the LORD; and the masons and the stonecutters. "…They gave the money which was weighed out into the hands of those who did the work, who had the oversight of the house of the LORD; and they paid it out to the carpenters and the builders who worked on the house of the LORD; and to the masons and the stonecutters, and for buying timber and hewn stone to repair the damages to the house of the LORD, and for all that was laid out for the house to repair it. But there were not made for the house of the LORD silver cups, snuffers, bowls, trumpets, any vessels of gold, or vessels of silver from the money which was brought into the house of the LORD." (2 Kings 12:11-15).

At the health facility salaries were paid by the last day of the month. So sometimes it would be on 28th, 29th, 30th or 31st, depending on the month. The book of Zechariah gives an illustration of two shepherds that paid Zecharia thirty pieces of silver. "…I told them, 'If you think it best, give me my pay; but if not, keep it.' So they paid me thirty pieces of silver." (Zechariah 11:12). According to the Book of 2 Kings and 2 Chronicles, King Josiah sent money which was to be delivered into the hand of the workmen who have the oversight of the house of the LORD, who were in turn to give it to the workmen who are in the house of the LORD to repair the damages of the house. "…Now in the eighteenth year of King Josiah, the king sent Shaphan, the son of Azaliah the son of Meshullam the scribe, to the house of the LORD saying, 'Go up to Hilkiah the high priest that he may count the money brought in to the house of the LORD which the doorkeepers have gathered from the people. Let them deliver it into the hand of the workmen who have the oversight of the house of the LORD, and let them give it to the workmen who are in the house of the LORD to repair the damages of the house…"(2 Kings 22:3-7 and 2 Chronicles 34:8-11).

I have witnessed many cases of employees who fail to have a savings plan or an investment plan and would end up spending all the money that they are paid. Some of those cases have ended up making their families suffer in the event of their demise. At the security company, we lost one of our employees and when it came to payment of the final dues, there was very little to be given out. The employee did not have any other savings elsewhere. I took it upon myself to organize with the Sacco team to come and sensitize employees on financial planning. Saving and investing is rewarding in the long run.

In the Gospel of Luke, Jesus tells his disciples the parable of a man of noble birth who went to a distant country to have himself appointed king and then return. The man called 10 of his servants and gave them 10 minas. He asked them to keep the money until his return. When he returned he sent for the servants to whom he had given the money, in order to find out what they had gained with it. The first one had earned 10 more and was put in charge of 10 cities. The second had earned five more and was put in charge of five cities. Then the last servant said he had kept the minas laid away in a piece of cloth because he was afraid of the king. The king asked those standing by to take his mina away from him and give it to the one who had 10 minas. When the king was asked why he did that he said that to everyone who has, more will be given, but as for the one who has nothing, even what they have will be taken away.

We see reward for the good job the first two servants did. "While they were listening to this, he went on to tell them a parable, because he was near Jerusalem and the people thought that the kingdom of God was going to appear at once. He said: 'A man of noble birth went to a distant country to have himself appointed king and then to return. So he called ten of his servants and gave them ten minas. Put this money to work,' he said, 'until I come back.' But his subjects hated him and sent a delegation after him to say, 'We don't want this man to be our king. 'He was made king, however, and returned home. Then he sent for the servants to whom he had given the money, in order to find out what they had gained with it. 'The first one came and said, 'Sir, your mina has earned ten more.' Well done, my good servant!' his master replied. 'Because you have been trustworthy in a very small matter, take charge of ten cities.' The second came and said, 'Sir, your mina has earned five more. His master answered, 'You take charge of five cities.' Then another servant came and said, 'Sir, here is your mina; I have kept it laid away in a piece of cloth. I was afraid of you, because you are a hard man. You take out what you did not put in and reap what you did not sow.' His master replied, 'I will judge you by your own words, you wicked servant! You knew, did you, that I am a hard man, taking out what I did not put in, and reaping what I did not sow? Why then didn't you put my money on deposit, so that when I came back, I could have collected it with interest?' Then he said to those standing by, 'Take his mina away from him and give it to the one who has ten minas.' Sir,' they said, 'he already has ten!' He replied, 'I tell you that to everyone who has, more will be given, but as for the one who has nothing, even what they have will be taken away. But those enemies of mine who did not want me to be king over them—bring them here and kill them in front of me." (Luke 19: 11-27).

When preparing an employment contract, the remuneration package will state the statutory deductions that will be made on the employee's salary. An employee can also give instructions to the human resource practitioner to make certain deductions. In my practice, I have made other deductions on employees' salaries in cases such as any amount advanced to an employee in excess of the amount of one month's wages of the employee; any amount due from the employee as a contribution to any provident fund; statutory deductions e.g. PAYE, NHIF, NSSF, HELB (where relevant) and any other statutory deduction as guided by the Laws of Kenya; no wages shall be payable to an employee in respect of a period during which the employee is detained in police custody or is serving a sentence of imprisonment imposed under any law; an amount in respect of each working day which the employee, without leave or other lawful cause, absents himself from work; an amount equal to the amount of any shortage of money arising through the negligence or dishonesty of an employee or unaccounted funds; an amount due and payable by the employee in accordance with the terms of an agreement in writing, by way of repayment or part repayment of a loan; and voluntary deductions: If authorized by the employee, the company may make deductions from his remuneration in respect of Sacco remittances and loans.

According to the Gospel of Matthew, employees ought to pay their taxes. "…They said, 'Caesar's.' Then he said to them, 'Therefore render to Caesar the things that are Caesar's, and to God the things that are

God's." (Matthew 22:21). According to the Gospel of Luke, John the Baptist told the soldiers not to take money from anyone by force, or accuse anyone falsely, and to be content with their wages. It is the duty of the human resource practitioner to pay the employees fairly. "Some soldiers were questioning him, saying, 'And what about us, what shall we do?' And he said to them, 'Do not take money from anyone by force, or accuse anyone falsely, and be content with your wages."(Luke 3:14).

Employees' salaries ought to be commensurate with the work they have done. In my experience, I have handled many cases of absenteeism. In cases where the behavior has become chronic, and the verbal warning has not borne any fruits, I have had to resort to treating the days they have been absent as unpaid. This means that the absent days are deducted in their salaries. The book of 2 Thessalonians gives an incident where Paul tells the believers that if anyone is not willing to work, then he is not to eat, either. "For even when we were with you, we used to give you this order: if anyone is not willing to work, then he is not to eat, either. For we hear that some among you are leading an undisciplined life, doing no work at all, but acting like busybodies. Now such persons we command and exhort in the Lord Jesus Christ to work in quiet fashion and eat their own bread." (2 Thessalonians 3:10-12).

Salaries will vary depending on the job title and the duties that one undertakes. At the security company, we had the salary structure divided into three categories. Category A was for senior management, Category B for middle-level management and Category C for frontline staff such as security guards, courier clerks, radio operators, among others. A security guard therefore would not earn the same salary as that of a senior manager. The book of Romans illustrates that God will repay each person according to what they have done. (Romans 2:6).

Senior management positions would have higher salaries and better benefit packages. At the media company, the senior managers had a better medical cover, fuel allowance, a company car, gym membership and club membership, among other benefits. The book of Nehemiah gives us an incident where Nehemiah says that in spite of all the work he had done, he never demanded the food allotted to the governor, because the demands were heavy on these people. This is to show that the governors had their own rewards. The position of a governor currently would call for a higher pay than that of a senator, for example. "…In spite of all this, I never demanded the food allotted to the governor, because the demands were heavy on these people." (Nehemiah 5:18).

According to the Gospel of John, Jesus says he is the true vine, and his Father is the gardener that cuts off every branch in him that bears no fruit, while every branch that does bear fruit he prunes so that it will be even more fruitful. "...I am the true vine, and my Father is the gardener. He cuts off every branch in me that bears no fruit, while every branch that does bear fruit he prunes so that it will be even more fruitful. You are already clean because of the word I have spoken to you." (John 15:1-3). The same message is brought out in the book of 2 Corinthians 5:10. It states, " For we must all appear before the judgment seat of Christ, so that each of us may receive what is due us for the things done while in the body, whether good or bad."

Before joining the human resource profession, I was a teacher and also did some sales jobs. In one of the schools I taught at in Nairobi's Eastlands, whenever it was end month, instead of the school paying out full salaries, we would be given a fraction of the salary in the name of advance. As a part time sales executive while I was still in college, the terms were that for the first three months I was to work from my own pocket without a salary. I was supposed to only get paid on commission. One time I brought in a cheque of Kshs.17,500 and upon submission I was not given my cut. I had no idea what do to do about these two cases and I let sleeping dogs lie. But what I tell my colleagues and other employees today is to never work on verbal agreements; let any form of engagement be in writing so that you can take legal action when an employer defrauds you. The book of Leviticus 19:13 states "Do not defraud or rob your neighbor. Do not hold back the wages of a hired worker overnight."

It is an employee's right to receive fair wages. All employers ought to display employees' rights where all employees are able to access and read them. At the security company, the employees' rights were attached to their name tags and fair wages was one of the rights. The book of 1 Timothy states the laborer deserves his wages. (1 Timothy 5:18) According to the book of Deuteronomy, God tells Moses not to oppress a hired servant who is poor and needy, and to give him his wages on his day before the sun sets. This shows that wages should be paid on time. "...You shall not oppress a hired servant who is poor and needy, whether he is one of your countrymen or one of your aliens who is in your land in your towns. You shall give him his wages on his day before the sun sets, for he is poor and sets his heart on it; so that he will not cry against you to the LORD and it becomes sin in you." (Deuteronomy 24:14-15).

According to the book of Malachi, the Lord says he will be quick to testify against sorcerers, adulterers and perjurers, against those who defraud laborers of their wages, who oppress the widows and the fatherless, and deprive the foreigners among you of justice. "…So I will come to put you on trial. I will be quick to testify against sorcerers, adulterers and perjurers, against those who defraud laborers of their wages, who oppress the widows and the fatherless, and deprive the foreigners among you of justice, but do not fear me," says the Lord Almighty." (Malachi 3:5) The book of James gives us an example where workers who had been defrauded of their wages cried and complained about it. "…Behold, the wages of the laborers who mowed your fields, which you kept back by fraud, are crying out against you, and the cries of the harvesters have reached the ears of the Lord of hosts." (James 5:4).

Jacob complains to Rachel and Leah about how their father had cheated him and changed his wages ten times. "You know that I have served your father with all my strength. Yet your father has cheated me and changed my wages ten times; however, God did not allow him to hurt me." (Genesis 31:6-7) Paul tells the masters in the book of Colossians to provide their slaves with what is right and fair, because they know that they also have a Master in heaven. "Masters, provide your slaves with what is right and fair, because you know that you also have a Master in heaven." (Colossians 4:1) At the health facility, there was an allowance for when one conducts interviews over the weekend. These monies would usually be given by cheque after the interview. In the book of Numbers, Moses receives instructions from God to tell the Levites that their households may eat the rest of the offering anywhere, for it is their wages for the work at the tent of meeting. (Numbers 18:31).

When an employee voluntarily resigns from his/her position, it is the duty of the human resource practitioner to ensure the employee is cleared smoothly and paid their final dues. At the security company, there was a service pay for staff who had worked for more than five years as an appreciation for their service. The book of Deuteronomy gives an example where the Lord tells Moses not to consider it a hardship to set his servant free, because the servant's service to him for six years has been worth twice as much as that of a hired hand. "Do not consider it a hardship to set your servant free, because their service to you these six years has been worth twice as much as that of a hired hand. And the LORD your God will bless you in everything you do." (Deuteronomy 15:18)

At the media company there was a case of a staff who had not taken his annual leave for about three years and had not been compensated, which is contrary to the law. When this employee was terminated, he sued the company for unfair termination and court ruled in his favour, and among the calculations for compensation was this accrued leave. The book of Jeremiah shows the consequences of unfair wages. "… Woe to him who builds his palace by unrighteousness, his upper rooms by injustice, making his own people work for nothing, not paying them for their labor." (Jeremiah 22:13).

According to the book of Leviticus, Moses talks of a seller and his purchaser calculating the payment from the year when he sold himself to him up to the year of jubilee; and the price of his sale corresponding to the number of years. Moses compares the seller to a hired man. "He then with his purchaser shall calculate from the year when he sold himself to him up to the year of jubilee; and the price of his sale shall correspond to the number of years. It is like the days of a hired man that he shall be with him."(Leviticus 25:50). This is a comparison to service pay. Reward follows good performance. At the media company and the health facility, we had end-of-year parties where we would recognize the best employee of the year, the best department of the year, the most improved employee, among others. The Gospel of Matthew illustrates that when you seek first the kingdom of God and his righteousness, all these things will be added to you. "But seek first the kingdom of God and his righteousness, and all these things will be added to you." (Matthew 6:33).

The Gospel of Matthew gives an example where a master congratulates his servant for being faithful over a little and sets him over much. "…His master said to him, 'Well done, good and faithful servant. You have been faithful over a little; I will set you over much. Enter into the joy of your master."(Matthew 25:23) In the end-year parties we would also reward the longest serving employees with vouchers or cheques to appreciate their loyalty. I learnt this practice at the banking institution and at the security company and introduced it at the health facility. The book of 1Samuel 26:23 states, "The LORD rewards everyone for their righteousness and faithfulness."

When I was at the security company, I received an award for the best performing Secretary of the Health and Safety Committee. The Gospel of John indicates that the reward for believers is eternal life. "For God so loved the world, that he gave his only Son, that whoever believes in him should not perish but have eternal life." (John 3:16) God's protection is one of the rewards for those who serve the Lord. According to the Gospel of Matthew, Peter received the protection of Jesus Christ against the gates of hell. "…And I tell you, you are Peter, and on this rock I will build my church, and the gates of hell shall not prevail against it." (Matthew 16:18) God's providence is another reward that is highlighted in the book of Proverbs. "…Honor the Lord with your wealth and with the first fruits of all your produce; then your barns will be filled with plenty, and your vats will be bursting with wine." (Proverbs 3:9-10) Salvation, according to the Gospel of Matthew, is a reward for endurance. "…But the one who endures to the end will be saved." (Matthew 24:13).

According to the book of Deuteronomy, exaltation is the reward for obedience. "…And if you faithfully obey the voice of the Lord your God, being careful to do all his commandments that I command you today, the Lord your God will set you high above all the nations of the earth. And all these blessings shall come upon you and overtake you, if you obey the voice of the Lord your God. Blessed shall you be in the city, and blessed shall you be in the field. Blessed shall be the fruit of your womb and the fruit of your ground and the fruit of your cattle, the increase of your herds and the young of your flock. Blessed shall be your basket and your kneading bowl…" (Deuteronomy 28:1-68).

When an employee fails to perform his/her duties as expected, he/she risks losing their job. One of the measures taken on poor performance is performance improvement plan. This is a warning for the staff to improve their performance within three months or they be terminated. Others include probationary termination, demotion etc. But when an employee is performing well they can be promoted, and they may also receive a performance related pay. The book of 2 Timothy gives an instance of the hardworking farmer, being the first to receive a share of the crops. "The hardworking farmer should be the first to receive a share of the crops." (2 Timothy 2:6).

At the media company, there was an employee who joined the company as a receptionist and as the years went by she went back to school and did CPA. This employee earned herself a promotion to the accounts department as a Cashier; she was later promoted to be a Receivables Accountant. At the security company we had many cases of staff who joined the company as security officers and were promoted after studies to branch managers, to trainers, and to supervisors. The book of 2 Corinthians illustrates that whoever sows sparingly will also reap sparingly, and whoever sows bountifully will also reap bountifully. "The point is this: whoever sows sparingly will also reap sparingly, and whoever sows bountifully will also reap bountifully." (2 Corinthians 9:6).

Commitment was one of the core values at the media company. If any employee expects to earn a salary then he/she must work for it. The book of Genesis 3:17-19 states, "...Listen to me; I give you the field, and I give you the cave that is in it. I give it to you in the presence of my people. Bury your dead."

When terminating an employment contract, the employer pays the staff for the number of years that the staff has served the employer. If the case is redundancy, then the employer pays the staff severance pay at a rate of 15 days for each completed year of service as guided by the Employment Act 2007. Jeremiah 22:13 states, "Woe to him who builds his house and uses his neighbor's services without pay; and does not give him his wages."

The book of Haggai gives an example of poor management of salaries when one has earned. "You have sown much, but harvest little; you eat, but there is not enough to be satisfied; you drink, but there is not enough to become drunk; you put on clothing, but no one is warm enough; and he who earns, earns wages to put into a purse with holes." (Haggai 1:6) This is very typical in a work environment. I have seen staff earning their salaries in the first week of the month and by the second week they are already asking for a salary advance or complaining that they are broke. Financial responsibility is vital among employed workers. According to the book of Zecharia, in the past there was no wage for man or any wage for animal. "For before those days there was no wage for man or any wage for animal; and for him who went out or came in there was no peace because of his enemies, and I set all men one against another." (Zechariah 8:10).

We have positions that we call "hard to find" in human resource management terms. These are positions whose salaries would not fall in the existing salary structure of an organization. At the media company, for example, we had seasoned radio presenters who we had poached from other media companies. Such employees' salaries would be determined by the market rate in the industry. As a company we would then offer them a slightly higher salary than the market rate. The same practice was adopted at the health facility. According to the book of 1 Kings 5:6 Solomon borrowed Hiram's servants at a rate that Hiram would quote. "…Now therefore, command that they cut for me cedars from Lebanon, and my servants will be with your servants; and I will give you wages for your servants according to all that you say, for you know that there is no one among us who knows how to cut timber like the Sidonians."

5.0 INDUSTRIAL RELATIONS

Industrial relations are a very key function of human resource management. It is the duty of the employer to ensure healthy industrial relations, ranging from relations and staff welfare, discipline management, grievance handling process, teamwork, and equal opportunity to all. In any given workplace there exist three types of relationships: Employer-Employee relationship; Employee-Employer relationship and Employee-Employee relationship.

Teamwork is one element that is vital in employee relations. At the media company we had team-building activities. At one point we took the staff to Sagana for three days for a team-building exercise. The activities of this event were centered on teamwork. At the health facility, team building was always in the human resource plan of each year. Employees would be taken to different places each year for at least one day for team-building activities.

According to the book of 1 Corinthians, Paul gives an example of the human body as how Christians are in Christ. He says Christians were all baptized by one Spirit so as to form one body. "…Just as a body, though one, has many parts, but all its many parts form one body, so it is with Christ. For we were all baptized by one Spirit so as to form one body—whether Jews or Gentiles, slave or free—and we were all given the one Spirit to drink. Even so the body is not made up of one part but of many. Now if the foot should say, 'Because I am not a hand, I do not belong to the body,' it would not for that reason stop being part of the body. And if the ear should say, 'Because I am not an eye, I do not belong to the body,' it would not for that reason stop being part of the body. If the whole body were an eye, where would the sense of hearing be? If the whole body were an ear, where would the sense of smell be? But in fact God has placed the parts in the body, every one of them, just as he wanted them to be. If they were all one part, where would the body be? As it is, there are many parts, but one body. The eye cannot say to the hand, 'I don't need you!' And the head cannot say to the feet, 'I don't need you!' On the contrary, those parts of the body that seem to be weaker are indispensable, and the parts that we think are less honorable we treat with special honor. And the parts that are unpresentable are treated with special modesty, while our presentable parts need no special treatment. But God has put the body together, giving greater honor to the parts that lacked it, so that there should be no division in the body, but that its parts should have equal concern for each other. If one part suffers, every part suffers with it; if one part is honored, every part rejoices with it. Now you are the body of Christ, and each one of you is a part of it. And God has placed in the church first of all apostles, second prophets, third teachers, then miracles, then gifts of healing, of helping, of guidance, and of different kinds of tongues. Are all apostles? Are all prophets? Are all teachers? Do all work miracles? Do all have gifts of healing? Do all speak in tongues? Do all interpret? Now eagerly desire the greater gifts." (1 Corinthians 12:12-31).

At the banking institution, we had a football team that was playing countrywide. This football team had employees from different departments. They exuded teamwork when they went to compete against other institutions.

Staff welfare is another element in employee relations. It is the duty of the human resource practitioner to see to it that the welfare of the employees is catered for. According to the Occupational Health and Safety Act 2007, Section 91 and 92, it is the duty of the employer to ensure the employee's safety, health and welfare. It states that, "(1)Every occupier shall provide and maintain an adequate supply of wholesome drinking water at suitable points conveniently accessible to all persons employed; (2) A supply of drinking water which is not laid on shall be contained in suitable vessels, and shall be renewed at least daily, and all practicable steps shall be taken to preserve the water and vessels from contamination, and a drinking water supply whether laid on or not shall, in such cases as an occupational safety and health officer may direct, be clearly indicated as the occupational safety and health officer may require; (3) Every occupier shall provide and maintain for the use of persons employed, adequate and suitable facilities for washing, which shall be conveniently accessible and shall be kept in a clean and orderly condition; (4) Every occupier shall provide and maintain for the use of a person employed, adequate and suitable accommodation for clothing not worn during working hours; (5) Every occupier shall provide and maintain, for the use of a person employed whose work is done standing, suitable facilities for sitting, sufficient to enable the person employed to take advantage of any opportunities for resting which may occur in the course of his employment, (6) Every occupier shall provide and maintain so as to be readily accessible, a first-aid box or cupboard of the prescribed standard."

Employers and employees also consider staff welfare in the concern for others within the organization. The book of Acts gives an example where a devout man, who feared God with his entire household, gave alms generously to the people, and prayed continually to God. "...A devout man who feared God with his entire household, gave alms generously to the people, and prayed continually to God."(Acts 10:2).

Among the Corporate Social Responsibilities at the health facility, every April and May of each year, employees would come together and bring clothing and foodstuff to be taken to an orphanage or to the home for the old. According to the book of Acts, Christians devoted themselves to the apostles' teaching and the fellowship, to the breaking of bread and the prayers. They sold their possessions and belongings and distributed the proceeds to all. "...And they devoted themselves to the apostles' teaching and the fellowship, to the breaking of bread and the prayers. And awe came upon every soul, and many wonders and signs were being done through the apostles. And all who believed were together and had all things in common. And they were selling their possessions and belongings and distributing the proceeds to all, as any had need. And day by day, attending the temple together and breaking bread in their homes, they received their food with glad and generous hearts..." (Acts 2:42-46).

When staffs show concern for each other there exists a harmonious relationship among them. The book of Psalms indicates that goodness will come to those who are generous and lend freely. "Good will come to those who are generous and lend freely, who conduct their affairs with justice." (Psalms 112:5). Christians, in the book of Romans, are urged to love one another. "...Owe no one anything, except to love each other, for the one who loves another has fulfilled the law." (Romans 13:8). At the health facility there was a time we lost one of our employees in an armed robbery incident in which the employee was stabbed to death. Other employees stood with their colleague's family from the date of the incident up to the time of burial. Employees would organize themselves in groups and go visit the bereaved family with some shopping for upkeep. During the funeral, many of the employees volunteered to travel about 350km to the home of the deceased where the burial took place.

The book of Deuteronomy gives us an example of where Moses requests the Israelites to be generous to one another. "If among you, one of your brothers should become poor, in any of your towns within your land that the Lord your God is giving you, you shall not harden your heart or shut your hand against your poor brother, but you shall open your hand to him and lend him sufficient for his need, whatever it may be. Take care lest there be an unworthy thought in your heart and you say, 'The seventh year, the year of release is near,' and your eye look grudgingly on your poor brother, and you give him nothing, and he cry to the Lord against you, and you be guilty of sin. You shall give to him freely, and your heart shall not be grudging when you give to him, because for this the Lord your God will bless you in all your work and in all that you undertake. For there will never cease to be poor in the land. Therefore I command you, 'You shall open wide your hand to your brother, to the needy and to the poor, in your land." (Deuteronomy 15:7-11); and Acts 20:35 states, "In all things I have shown you that by working hard in this way we must help the weak and remember the words of the Lord Jesus, how he himself said, 'It is more blessed to give than to receive."

According to the book of Colossians, Paul urges Christians to put on holy and beloved, compassionate hearts, kindness, humility, meekness, and patience. "...Put on then, as God's chosen ones, holy and beloved, compassionate hearts, kindness, humility, meekness, and patience, bearing with one another and, if one has a complaint against another, forgiving each other; as the Lord has forgiven you, so you also must forgive. And above all these put on love, which binds everything together in perfect harmony."(Colossians 3:12-14). At the health facility there was a staff who had a sick child at home. The child had undergone numerous surgeries and exhausted the employee's medical cover. This staff requested her colleagues to help her raise funds for the last operation which would correct the child's problem permanently. Staff contributed very well in cash and others signed a pledge form to have a certain amount deducted from their salaries towards this course.

Paul goes on to urge Christians in the book of Ephesians to put off falsehood and speak truthfully to their neighbor. He urges them to get rid of all bitterness, rage and anger, brawling and slander, along with every form of malice; and to be kind and compassionate to one another, forgiving each other, just as in Christ God forgave them. "… Therefore each of you must put off falsehood and speak truthfully to your neighbor, for we are all members of one body. 'In your anger do not sin': Do not let the sun go down while you are still angry, and do not give the devil a foothold. Anyone who has been stealing must steal no longer, but must work, doing something useful with their own hands, that they may have something to share with those in need. Do not let any unwholesome talk come out of your mouths, but only what is helpful for building others up according to their needs, that it may benefit those who listen. And do not grieve the Holy Spirit of God, with whom you were sealed for the day of redemption. Get rid of all bitterness, rage and anger, brawling and slander, along with every form of malice. Be kind and compassionate to one another, forgiving each other, just as in Christ God forgave you." (Ephesians 4:25-32).

The books of James, Matthew, John, Luke, 2 Corinthians, Philippians and Romans carry the message of concern for others, helping the poor and generosity. Philippians 2: 2-8 states, "What good is it, my brothers, if someone says he has faith but does not have works? Can that faith save him? If a brother or sister is poorly clothed and lacking in daily food, and one of you says to them, 'Go in peace, be warmed and filled,' without giving them the things needed for the body, what good is that? So also faith by itself, if it does not have works, is dead. But someone will say, 'You have faith and I have works.' Show me your faith apart from your works, and I will show you my faith by my works . . ."; Proverbs 14:21 states, "Whoever despises his neighbor is a sinner, but blessed is he who is generous to the poor."; 2 Corinthians 9:7 states, "Each one must give as he has decided in his heart, not reluctantly or under compulsion, for God loves a cheerful giver."; John 13:34-35 states, "A new commandment I give to you, that you love one another: just as I have loved you, you also are to love one another. By this all people will know that you are my disciples, if you have love for one another." James 2:8 states, "If you really fulfill the royal law according to the Scripture, 'You shall love your neighbor as yourself', you are doing well." Luke 6:38 states, "Give, and it will be given to you. Good measure, pressed down, shaken together, running over, will be put into your lap. For with the measure you use it will be measured back to you."

According to the Gospel of Matthew generous people will be recognized in the kingdom of God. "When the Son of Man comes in his glory, and all the angels with him, then he will sit on his glorious throne. Before him will be gathered all the nations, and he will separate people one from another as a shepherd separates the sheep from the goats. And he will place the sheep on his right, but the goats on the left. Then the King will say to those on his right, 'Come, you who are blessed by my Father, inherit the kingdom prepared for you from the foundation of the world. For I was hungry and you gave me food, I was thirsty and you gave me drink, I was a stranger and you welcomed me." (Matthew 25:31-46); Matthew 22:34-40 states, "But when the Pharisees heard that he had silenced the Sadducees, they gathered together. And one of them, a lawyer, asked him a question to test him. 'Teacher, which is the great commandment in the Law?' And he said to him, 'You shall love the Lord your God with all your heart and with all your soul and with your entire mind. This is the great and first commandment' . . ."; and Matthew 5:42 states, "Give to the one who begs from you, and do not refuse the one who would borrow from you."

In the disciplinary code, gossip, falsehood and slander all fall under disciplinary offences. Employees are therefore urged to peacefully co-exist with one another. At the security company, there was a staff who started a rumor that the Courier Supervisor was dating a senior manager. This rumor did not have any basis and it was against a senior manager. The staff who started the rumor was brought into my office and I gave her a warning letter for spreading malicious rumors. I also handled another case of gossip at the health facility where a nurse happened to have made a statement to mean that one of the doctors was dating her boss. This statement led to rumors spreading that the doctor's office had a bed and was acting as a multipurpose room to mean that the doctor had loose morals. When the doctor brought the case to my attention, I called the nurse in question and asked her to explain herself.

I then asked her to write a formal apology letter to the doctor and to refrain from gossip moving forward.

According to the book of Leviticus; Matthew, and Romans, Christians are called upon to forgive each other. In a workplace it is normal to have some disagreements in the course of performing duties but the disagreements are not supposed to graduate to grudges. Employees should learn to peacefully co-exist among themselves. I have handled a number of cases where at the end of the hearing I would ask the staff to shake hands and forgive each other. "You have heard that it was said, 'An eye for an eye and a tooth for a tooth.' But I say to you, do not resist the one who is evil. But if anyone slaps you on the right cheek, turn to him the other also. And if anyone would sue you and take your tunic, let him have your cloak as well."(Matthew 5:38-40); "…You shall not take vengeance or bear a grudge against the sons of your own people, but you shall love your neighbor as yourself: I am the Lord." (Leviticus 19:18); and Romans 12:17-21 states "… Repay no one evil for evil, but give thought to do what is honorable in the sight of all. If possible, so far as it depends on you, live peaceably with all. Beloved, never avenge yourselves, but leave it to the wrath of God, for it is written, "Vengeance is mine, I will repay, says the Lord.' To the contrary, 'if your enemy is hungry, feed him; if he is thirsty, give him something to drink; for by so doing you will heap burning coals on his head.' Do not be overcome by evil, but overcome evil with good."

Responsibility and accountability are outlined in the book of 2 Thessalonians and Psalms. I have seen a number of employees complain about their fellow employees. A case in point is when an employee requests his/her colleague to guarantee them when seeking a loan from a Sacco then the colleague is either dismissed or they resign without paying up the loan, leaving the guarantor with the burden of clearing the loan. This is an example of someone taking advantage of another's generosity. "…Now we command you, brothers, in the name of our Lord Jesus Christ that you keep away from any brother who is walking in idleness and not in accord with the tradition that you received from us. For you yourselves know how you ought to imitate us, because we were not idle when we were with you, nor did we eat anyone's bread without paying for it, but with toil and labor we worked night and day, that we might not be a burden to any of you. It was not because we do not have that right, but to give you in ourselves an example to imitate.

For even when we were with you, we would give you this command: If anyone is not willing to work, let him not eat . . ." (2 Thessalonians 3:6-12); and "The wicked borrows but does not pay back, but the righteous is generous and gives..." (Psalms 37:21).

According to the Gospel of Matthew, Christians are reminded to treat others as they would wish to be treated if they were in the same circumstances. "...So whatever you wish that others would do to you, do also to them, for this is the Law and the Prophets." (Matthew 7:12). At the health facility I handled a case in which one staff reported that her colleagues in the department treated her like a plague. They avoided her at all times and mocked her. I also had a similar case of a male staff of high integrity who would be mistreated by the rest of his colleagues in the department because he would not see indiscipline and fail to report. In both cases I convened a meeting with the entire department and asked them to explain why they mistreat their colleagues. At the end of the meeting the employees would shake hands as a sign of reconciliation.

Employees ought to behave well while at work to maintain a proper employee-employer relationship. At the media company, there was an incident of a newspaper sales executive who sold advertising space to a client but did not place the advertisement. The client paid this sales executive directly. The following day, the client came to complain to the company why his advertisement had not been published in the newspaper. By this time, the culprit had taken to his heels and was nowhere to be seen. He had switched off his phone and all efforts to contact him were futile. This is a case of an employee defrauding a client and the employer because the company had to run at a loss publishing an advertisement the following day without being paid to maintain good customer relations. The book of Proverbs advises Christians to earn their money honestly. "Better a little with righteousness than much gain with injustice." (Proverbs 16:8).

The book of Deuteronomy gives us an instance where servants are asked to be honest while performing their duties. Moses tells the Israelites not to have two differing weights in their bags. "...Do not have two differing weights in your bag—one heavy, one light. Do not have two differing measures in your house—one large, one small. You must have accurate and honest weights and measures, so that you may live long in the land the Lord your God is giving you." (Deuteronomy

25:13-15). At the media company, we hired an internal auditor who was able to flag fraudulent entries in the books of accounts. The Chief Accountant and his deputy committed fraud of over Ksh7 million. The payroll list had many ghost workers and some of the names of the workers were actually the wives of these two employees. When it was flagged they were suspended and they decided not to show up for their disciplinary hearing. They had embezzled a lot of money and had started a business, built rental apartments and bought cars. We decided to have the matter handled by our company lawyer.

At the health facility there were many cases of receipts forgery and general fraud. One department was notorious in this offence. When I joined the facility I was given the history of the department and it appeared that it had been the norm of the department to commit fraud. One incident that happened before I joined the facility was that the head of department and one employee stole equipment from the department and would also poach patients while attending to them. A patient would be told to go to their private clinic for review. When I joined the facility, these employees had been fired and new ones recruited. A few months down the line, a client complained about poor quality services and fraud. This client was a pastor. He came to ask why he had not been issued with a receipt for the services he had received. On investigation, the head of department was the one who had committed fraud and when I gave her a show cause letter, she texted the pastor asking him not to sell her out. The employee did not know that this client was a pastor. I invited the pastor to come and give his side of the story and when he was still in my office, I called in this head of department. When she came and saw the pastor she ran away and never showed up at work again.

Employees ought to obey the instructions of their supervisors because they speak with the authority of the management of an organization. In the book of Hebrews, Paul tells believers to have confidence in their leaders and to submit to their authority. "Have confidence in your leaders and submit to their authority, because they keep watch over you as those who must give an account. Do this so that their work will be a joy, not a burden, for that would be of no benefit to you." (Hebrews 13:17). At the security company I was in charge of 1,000 frontline staff, including security officers and their supervisors. In the day-to-day running of operations, some security guards would fall sick and warrant a replacement at the duty station. Some of the complaints that I received from the supervisors were that a security guard had been requested to change his/her shift to cover for the one who was sick but they refused to do so. This is referred to as insubordination in the Employment Act 2007. Failure to obey lawful instructions is gross misconduct and amounts to summary dismissal.

According to the book of Ephesians, it is important for slaves to obey their earthly masters with fear and trembling, with a sincere heart, as they would Christ. "Slaves, obey your earthly masters with fear and trembling, with a sincere heart, as you would Christ, not by the way of eye-service, as people-pleasers, but as servants of Christ, doing the will of God from the heart, rendering service with a good will as to the Lord and not to man, knowing that whatever good anyone does, this he will receive back from the Lord, whether he is a slave or free." (Ephesians 6:5-8). At the health facility, a machine once broke down but the staff on duty failed to report it to the supervisor. This caused a lot of delays in other processes and when the staff was asked they became defensive. The procedure for when a machine broke down was to inform the supervisor and if the supervisor was not on site then they were to report to the next available line of authority.

Respect and fairness was one of the core values at the health facility. This value was among the employee rights at the security company as well. According to the book of 1 Timothy, Christians are expected to respect the elderly and give proper recognition to the needy. "…Do not rebuke an older man harshly, but exhort him as if he were your father. Treat younger men as brothers, older women as mothers, and younger women as sisters, with absolute purity. Give proper recognition to those widows who are really in need. But if a widow has children or grandchildren, these should learn first of all to put their religion into practice by caring for their own family and so repaying their parents and grandparents, for this is pleasing to God." (1 Timothy 5:1-4). All employees are expected to respect their colleagues, supervisors, and heads of departments, line managers and top-level managers. Sometimes a supervisor may be wrong but the employee should not embarrass the supervisor in public. They can call them aside and correct them. This is likely to happen when you are supervising staff in an area that you are not an expert and you are bound to say one or two things that may not be as the technical team would have put it.

When an employee reports to work, they are given company equipment to assist them in performing their duties. The employees are expected to take personal responsibility and not lose these equipment. At the media company, almost all staff were given laptops when they reported to work. These laptops were to be used only within the company and if there was need for the staff to carry away the laptop, they would sign an asset movement form. When an employee lost the laptop, for example, they would be required to pay for it. The book of 1 Peter gives an illustration of how Christians are called upon to use whatever gift they have received to serve others, as faithful stewards of God's grace in its various forms. "Each of you should use whatever gift you have received to serve others, as faithful stewards of God's grace in its various forms." (1 Peter 4:10).

Employers are also expected to treat their employees fairly. Employers could also refer to managers and supervisors. In my practice I have developed human resource policies, including equal opportunity policy. This policy states that all staff will be treated fairly and that policy will apply across the board without any discrimination. The Employment Act 2007 Section 5 warns employers against discrimination based on race, gender, marital status, religious status, language, political opinion, ethnic or social origin, disability, pregnancy, mental status or HIV status. According to the book of Job it is not right to deny justice to any servants, whether male or female. "…If I have denied justice to any of my servants, whether male or female, when they had a grievance against me, what will I do when God confronts me? What will I answer when called to account?" (Job 31:13-14).

The book of Proverbs advises Christians against oppression of the poor. "One who oppresses the poor to increase his wealth and one who gives gifts to the rich—both come to poverty." (Proverbs 22:16). Employers should not mistreat their employees. The book of Deuteronomy illustrates the importance of fairness in a dispute resolution. "…And I charged your judges at that time, 'hear the disputes between your people and judge fairly, whether the case is between two Israelites or between an Israelite and a foreigner residing among you. Do not show partiality in judging; hear both small and great alike. Do not be afraid of anyone, for judgment belongs to God. Bring me any case too hard for you, and I will hear it.' And at that time I told you everything you were to do."(Deuteronomy 1:16-18).

According to the book of Colossians, masters should treat their slaves justly and fairly. "Masters, treat your slaves justly and fairly, knowing that you also have a Master in heaven." (Colossians 4:1). When I joined the health facility, there was no salary structure. One of the tasks I undertook to perform in the first three months was to conduct an employee survey. The result of the survey indicated that there were a lot of salary discrepancies. Employees with the same qualifications and experience were getting different salaries. The employees would say salary reviews were based on favoritism. With the support of top-level management, I embarked on the process of establishing job groups and salary structures to mitigate this problem.

Managers and supervisors ought to train staff on how to perform the tasks because different companies have different ways of doing things. New staff must be oriented into the organization's culture. At the health facility from time to time we would engage nurses on temporary basis to work in cases where we had an influx in patient numbers. There was a case in June 2017 where a new nurse was tasked to take a patient from the surgical ward to the theatre. This nurse walked the patient to the theatre which was contrary to the practice at the health facility. The practice was that a patient was supposed to be wheeled to the theater, with IV fluids injected on them. When the nurse was probed about the incident, she said that the practice was different at the hospital where she had worked prior to joining this facility. She was then taken through the procedures and protocols in the new work place.

According to the book of Exodus, Moses received instructions from Jethro to teach the Israelites God's decrees and instructions, and show them the way they are to live and how they are to behave. "…Teach them his decrees and instructions, and show them the way they are to live and how they are to behave. But select capable men from all the people—men who fear God, trustworthy men who hate dishonest gain—and appoint them as officials over thousands, hundreds, fifties and tens. Have them serve as judges for the people at all times, but have them bring every difficult case to you; the simple cases they can decide themselves. That will make your load lighter, because they will share it with you. If you do this and God so commands, you will be able to stand the strain, and all these people will go home satisfied.' Moses listened to his father-in-law and did everything he said. He chose capable men from all Israel and made them leaders of the people, officials over thousands, hundreds, fifties and tens. They served as judges for the people at all times. The difficult cases they brought to Moses, but the simple ones they decided themselves."(Exodus 18:20-26).

At the media company, sales executives and ICT staff would complain that their bosses had threatened to sack them. They were worried about their job security. The book of Ephesians warns masters against threatening their servants. "Masters, do the same to them, and stop your threatening, knowing that he who is both their Master and yours is in heaven, and that there is no partiality with him." (Ephesians 6:9). At the health facility, a member of the senior management team was reported to have threatened to fire all staff because of one mistake that had been made. This resulted in low morale among these employees.

When policies are developed, they target everyone in the organization and not just the junior staff. Therefore managers ought to comply with the policies as well. According to the Gospel of Matthew, Luke and the book of Romans, masters should be role models to their servants. They should practice what they preach. ". . . You hypocrites! Well did Isaiah prophesy of you, when he said: 'These people honor me with their lips, but their heart is far from me; in vain do they worship me, teaching as doctrines the commandments of men.'?" (Matthew 15:7-9); Romans 2:21-24 states, "...You then who teach others, do you not teach yourself? While you preach against stealing, do you steal? You who say that one must not commit adultery, do you commit adultery? You who abhor idols, do you rob temples? You who boast in the law dishonor God by breaking the law. For, as it is written, 'The name of God is blasphemed among the Gentiles because of you'."; Luke 20:46-47 states, "Beware of the scribes, who like to walk around in long robes, and love greetings in the marketplaces and the best seats in the synagogues and the places of honor at feasts, who devour widows' houses and for a pretense make long prayers. They will receive the greater condemnation." and Matthew 7:15-20 states, "Beware of false prophets, who come to you in sheep's clothing but inwardly are ravenous wolves. You will recognize them by their fruits. Are grapes gathered from thorn bushes, or figs from thistles? So, every healthy tree bears good fruit, but the diseased tree bears bad fruit. A healthy tree cannot bear bad fruit, nor can a diseased tree bear good fruit. Every tree that does not bear good fruit is cut down and thrown into the fire . . ."

The Labor Relations Act 2007 gives guidance on how disputes are to be resolved. There must be mediation, reconciliation and arbitration if both the employer's and employee's representatives have failed to agree. In my practice, I have developed grievance handling procedures, which state that if employees have a dispute among themselves, they can report it to their immediate supervisor after they have failed to amicably agree, if the immediate supervisor is not able to resolve the matter, it is then forwarded to the line manager. If after the line manager has addressed the matter, but it is still not resolved, the case is brought to the human resource practitioner who will handle it or involve the Chief Executive Officer for a final decision. At the media company, there was an incident where a senior manager was publicly embarrassed by the Managing Director. This senior manager looked at the incident as disrespect and decided to resign. The Managing Director ought to have called the senior manager aside and corrected him privately instead of doing it in front of other junior employees.

I have received numerous grievances in my practice; some have been on sexual harassment, others on disrespect and use of abusive language by fellow employees or a senior manager, intimidation and victimization by managers, among others. I have successfully resolved all cases brought to my attention. I have seen instances among my professional colleagues in a human resource practitioners group on LinkedIn, where it is the top-level manager who has victimized or threatened a staff and the human resource practitioner is seeking advice from the rest on how to handle such a case. This can be quite challenging. The human resource practitioner can try to address it with the top-level manager in a friendly environment, or have a general talk with all managers, indirectly addressing the issues, or find a fellow manager who is close to the manager in question and ask them to talk to them.

Discipline management is part of the larger employee relations arm of human resource management. A disciplinary policy will outline the disciplinary code of the organization, indicating what offence is equal to which disciplinary measure. The purpose of a disciplinary policy is to keep employees' behavior in check while at work. Some of the disciplinary measures include verbal warnings/reprimands, cautionary letters, first warning letter, second warning letter, final warning letter, summary dismissal, penalties, suspension and demotion.

In my experience I have encountered many disciplinary offences such as absenteeism, lateness, intoxication, negligence, theft, fraud, insubordination, moonlighting, conflict of interest, use of abusive language, sleeping while on duty and breach of employment contract. At the media company, there was an incident where a radio presenter had been enlisted to host a show in another radio station. This was conflict of interest, and when she presented the letter to us we declined her request based on our disciplinary code.

At the security company I handled many cases of security guards sleeping while on duty. Other cases involved security guards colluding with thugs to rob a place of work and reporting to work while drunk. The trend was that after salaries were paid some security guards would not report to work for one or two days. And when they did they would usually be drunk. The trend was the same with one particular staff in the clinical department at the health facility. At the security company, there was an incident where thugs had dressed in our company's uniforms and called out the names of the security guards. There was also a case of a security guard stealing from a client, a bakery. The guard stole bread and took it home. The books of 1 Corinthians, 1 Timothy, Exodus, and Revelation provide a list of some of the offences. "...Or do you not know that the unrighteous will not inherit the kingdom of God? Do not be deceived: neither the sexually immoral, nor idolaters, nor adulterers, nor men who practice homosexuality, nor thieves, nor the greedy, nor drunkards, nor revilers, nor swindlers will inherit the kingdom of God. And such were some of you. But you were washed, you were sanctified, you were justified in the name of the Lord Jesus Christ and by the Spirit of our God." (1 Corinthians 6:9-11); 1 Timothy 1:10 states, "The sexually immoral, men who practice homosexuality, enslavers, liars, perjurers, and whatever else is contrary to sound doctrine."

The book of Leviticus warns Christians against committing disciplinary offences. "Do not steal, do not lie. Do not deceive one another." (Leviticus 19:11). The Gospel of Luke gives an example of Jesus warning tax collectors against extortion of money and asking them to be contented with their wages. "Tax collectors also came to be baptized and said to him, 'Teacher, what shall we do?' And he said to them, 'Collect no more than you are authorized to do.' Soldiers also asked him, 'And we, what shall we do?' And he said to them, "Do not extort money from anyone by threats or by false accusation, and be content with your wages." (Luke 3:12-14)

According to the book of Numbers, the Lord sent venomous snakes among the Israelites which bit the people and many Israelites died as a result of their sins. However, He forgave the ones who asked for forgiveness. "They traveled from Mount Hor along the route to the Red Sea, to go around Edom. But the people grew impatient on the way; they spoke against God and against Moses, and said, 'Why have you brought us up out of Egypt to die in the wilderness? There is no bread! There is no water! And we detest this miserable food!' Then the LORD sent venomous snakes among them; they bit the people and many Israelites died. The people came to Moses and said, 'We sinned when we spoke against the LORD and against you. Pray that the LORD will take the snakes away from us.' So Moses prayed for the people. The LORD said to Moses, 'Make a snake and put it up on a pole; anyone who is bitten can look at it and live.' So Moses made a bronze snake and put it up on a pole. Then when anyone was bitten by a snake and looked at the bronze snake, they lived." (Numbers 21: 4-9). This shows that when one commits an offence they are disciplined for it and when they own up to their mistake, they are forgiven.

In human resource practice, there are three written warnings that a staff can receive; a first warning, a second warning and a final warning, depending on the offence they have. The subsequent warnings are for offences that occur within 12 months from the date the first warning was given, whether or not the offences are related, as guided by the Employment Act 2007. Offences such as absence from work, lateness, abuse of sick leave policy, failure to complete handover procedure and dress code will warrant a first warning. Offences such as intoxication, sexual harassment, fraud, arrest for more than 14 days and gross negligence would result to summary dismissal. Just like for every cause there is an effect, for every action there is a reaction, all wrong doings have their consequences, according to the book of Philippians. "...For many, of whom I have often told you and now tell you even with tears, walk as enemies of the cross of Christ. Their end is destruction, their god is their belly, and they glory in their shame, with minds set on earthly things." (Philippians 3:18-19).

According to the book of Proverbs, the Lord detests dishonest scales. "The Lord detests dishonest scales, but accurate weights find favor with him." (Proverbs 11:1) Dishonesty is a disciplinary offence. I have handled many cases of dishonesty where a staff lies to a client or they lie about having performed their tasks as required or even lying about the charges for services and defrauding clients. Such staffs have always faced disciplinary action as per the organization's disciplinary procedure. At the health facility, there was a staff in the accounts department who used to charge clients different amounts and issue receipts while blocking the carbon copy, and then later on write by hand a different amount on the receipt book carbon copy. When this was discovered the employee was summarily dismissed. The gospel of Luke 16:10-12 states, "One who is faithful in a very little is also faithful in much, and one who is dishonest in a very little is also dishonest in much. If then you have not been faithful in the unrighteous wealth, who will entrust to you the true riches? And if you have not been faithful in that which is another's, who will give you that which is your own?"

According to the Gospel of Matthew and the books of 2 Peter, Romans and Proverbs, Christians are warned against dishonesty. "… Dishonest money dwindles away, but whoever gathers money little by little makes it grow."(Proverbs 13:11); 2 Peter 2:1-3 states, "But false prophets also arose among the people, just as there will be false teachers among you, who will secretly bring in destructive heresies, even denying the Master who bought them, bringing upon themselves swift destruction. And many will follow their sensuality, and because of them the way of truth will be blasphemed. And in their greed they will exploit you with false words. Their condemnation from long ago is not idle, and their destruction is not asleep."; Romans 16:18 states, "… For such persons do not serve our Lord Christ, but their own appetites, and by smooth talk and flattery they deceive the hearts of the naive."; Matthew 24:24 states, "…For false Christ's and false prophets will arise and perform great signs and wonders, so as to lead astray, if possible, even the elect."

According to the book of Exodus, if one steals, he must pay for it. "If a man steals an ox or a sheep, and kills it or sells it, he shall repay five oxen for an ox, and four sheep for a sheep. If a thief is found breaking in and is struck so that he dies, there shall be no blood guilt for him, but if the sun has risen on him, there shall be blood guilt for him. He shall surely pay. If he has nothing, then he shall be sold for his theft. If the stolen beast is found alive in his possession, whether it is an ox or a donkey or a sheep, he shall pay double. "If a man causes a field or vineyard to be grazed over, or lets his beast loose and it feeds in another man's field, he shall make restitution from the best in his own field and in his own vineyard . . ." (Exodus 22:1-31).

According to the book of Proverbs, negligence could lead to death. This, in human resource management, may be equivalent to gross negligence, which according to the Employment Act 2007, is gross misconduct and amounts to summary dismissal. For example, in the health facility, if a patient died because of a medic's gross negligence then the medic would be summarily dismissed. "The craving of a sluggard will be the death of him, because his hands refuse to work." (Proverbs 21:25).

According to the Gospel of Mark and the book of Titus, the consequence of lying and not believing in Christ is self-condemnation. The scripture talks of warning people twice then after that have nothing to do with them. "Warn a divisive person once, and then warn them a second time. After that, have nothing to do with them. You may be sure that such people are warped and sinful; they are self-condemned." (Titus 3:10-11); and Mark 16:16 states, "Whoever believes and is baptized will be saved, but whoever does not believe will be condemned."

The book of Hosea gives us an example of Samaria bearing her guilt, because she had rebelled against her God; and the people of Samaria falling by the sword; their little ones being dashed in pieces, and their pregnant women ripped open. (Hosea 13:16). This is to show that every disciplinary offence has a consequence. According to the Gospel of Luke, demotion can also be a consequence of a disciplinary offence. "And he called him and said to him, 'What is this that I hear about you? Turn in the account of your management, for you can no longer be manager." (Luke 16:2). This person was demoted for having forged receipts.

According to the Gospel of Matthew, it is an offence to serve two masters and to use abusive language. In the Employment Act 2007 Section 44, use of abusive language amounts to gross misconduct and the disciplinary action for such is summary dismissal. "No one can serve two masters, for either he will hate the one and love the other, or he will be devoted to the one and despise the other. You cannot serve God and money." (Matthew 6:24) and Matthew 5:21-26 states, "You have heard that it was said to those of old, 'You shall not murder; and whoever murders will be liable to judgment.' But I say to you that everyone who is angry with his brother will be liable to judgment; whoever insults his brother will be liable to the council; and whoever says, 'You fool!' will be liable to the hell of fire. So if you are offering your gift at the altar and there remember that your brother has something against you, leave your gift there before the altar and go. First be reconciled to your brother, and then come and offer your gift. Come to terms quickly with your accuser while you are going with him to court, lest your accuser hand you over to the judge, and the judge to the guard, and you be put in prison . . ."

The book of Joshua gives an instance where the Lord tells Joshua that the Israelites had sinned; they had transgressed God's covenant; they had taken some of the devoted things; they had stolen and lied and put them among their own belongings; they had become devoted for destruction and as a result God was going to abandon them unless they turned their ways. "... The Lord said to Joshua, 'Get up! Why have you fallen on your face? Israel has sinned; they have transgressed my covenant that I commanded them; they have taken some of the devoted things; they have stolen and lied and put them among their own belongings. Therefore the people of Israel cannot stand before their enemies. They turn their backs before their enemies, because they have become devoted for destruction. I will be with you no more, unless you destroy the devoted things from among you. Get up! Consecrate the people and say, 'Consecrate yourselves for tomorrow; for thus says the Lord, God of Israel, 'There are devoted things in your midst, O Israel. You cannot stand before your enemies until you take away the devoted things from among you.' In the morning therefore you shall be brought nearby your tribes. And the tribe that the Lord takes by lot shall come nearby clans. And the clan that the Lord takes shall come nearby households. And the household that the Lord takes shall come near man by man . . ." (Joshua 7:10-26).

In my practice, once employee indiscipline has been reported, I always issue a show cause letter to the employee, asking them to explain what happened. The disciplinary action for the offence would usually depend on how the employee responds to the show cause letter and the investigation report into the case. An employee can also write a statement narrating the chronology of events leading to the indiscipline.

The disciplinary process is outlined in the book of Deuteronomy. "If a man or woman living among you in one of the towns the LORD gives you is found doing evil in the eyes of the LORD your God in violation of his covenant, and contrary to my command has worshiped other gods, bowing down to them or to the sun or the moon or the stars in the sky, and this has been brought to your attention, then you must investigate it thoroughly. If it is true and it has been proved that this detestable thing has been done in Israel, take the man or woman who has done this evil deed to your city gate and stone that person to death. On the testimony of two or three witnesses a person is to be put to death, but no one is to be put to death on the testimony of only one witness. The hands of the witnesses must be the first in putting that person to death, and then the hands of all the people. You must purge the evil from among you. If cases come before your courts that are too difficult for you to judge—whether bloodshed, lawsuits or assaults—take them to the place the LORD your God will choose. Go to the Levitical priests and to the judge who is in office at that time. Inquire of them and they will give you the verdict." (Deuteronomy 17:2-8)

The book of Deuteronomy 19:16-19 states, "If a malicious witness takes the stand to accuse someone of a crime, the two people involved in the dispute must stand in the presence of the LORD before the priests and the judges who are in office at the time. The judges must make a thorough investigation, and if the witness proves to be a liar, giving false testimony against a fellow Israelite, then do to the false witness as that witness intended to do to the other party."

The purpose for discipline management is to correct a wrongdoing and to ensure that staffs adhere to the organization's policy. This is outlined in the books of Deuteronomy; Job; Psalm; Proverbs; Romans; Ephesians; Hebrews; and Revelation 3:19. All discipline may seem painful rather than pleasant, but later it yields the peaceful fruit of righteousness to those who have been trained by it. "For the moment all discipline seems painful rather than pleasant, but later it yields the peaceful fruit of righteousness to those who have been trained by it." (Hebrews 12:11); Proverbs 12:1 states, "Whoever loves discipline loves knowledge, but he who hates reproof is stupid."; Proverbs 13:24 states, "Whoever spares the rod hates his son, but he who loves him is diligent to discipline him."; Proverbs 23:13 states, "Do not withhold discipline from a child; if you punish them with the rod, they will not die."; Proverbs 29:17 states, "Discipline your children, and they will give you peace; they will bring you the delights you desire."; Proverbs 22:15 states,

"Folly is bound up in the heart of a child, but the rod of discipline will drive it far away."; Proverbs 13:1 states, "A wise son heeds his father's instruction, but a mocker does not respond to rebukes."; and Psalms 94:12-14 states, "Blessed is the one you discipline, Lord, the one you teach from your law; you grant them relief from days of trouble, till a pit is dug for the wicked. For the Lord will not reject his people; he will never forsake his inheritance."

Discipline management can also be used as a positive reinforcement of good behavior. According to the book of Titus, an elder must be hospitable, one who loves what is good, is self-controlled, upright, holy and disciplined. "Rather, he must be hospitable, one who loves what is good, and who is self-controlled, upright, holy and disciplined." (Titus 1:8). The book of Ecclesiastes gives an advice to employees on discipline. "…If a ruler's anger rises against you, do not leave your post; calmness can lay great offenses to rest." (Ecclesiastes 10:4). According to the book of Isaiah, obedience is rewarding. "…If you are willing and obedient, you shall eat the good of the land…" (Isaiah 1:19). The book of 2 Timothy illustrates that when you obey the rules and regulations you will be rewarded. "…Share in suffering as a good soldier of Christ Jesus. No soldier gets entangled in civilian pursuits, since his aim is to please the one who enlisted him. An athlete is not crowned unless he competes according to the rules." (2 Timothy 2:3-5).

According to the Gospel of Luke and the books of Romans, Hebrews and Proverbs, whoever resists the authorities resists what God has appointed, and those who resist will incur judgment. "…Let every person be subject to the governing authorities. For there is no authority except from God, and those that exist have been instituted by God. Therefore whoever resists the authorities resists what God has appointed, and those who resist will incur judgment. For rulers are not a terror to good conduct, but to bad. Would you have no fear of the one who is in authority? Then do what is good, and you will receive his approval, for he is God's servant for your good. But if you do wrong, be afraid, for he does not bear the sword in vain. For he is the servant of God, an avenger who carries out God's wrath on the wrongdoer. Therefore one must be in subjection, not only to avoid God's wrath but also for the sake of conscience." (Romans 13:1-14); Hebrews 13:17 states "Obey your leaders and submit to them, for they are keeping watch over your souls, as those who will have to give an account. Let them do this with joy and not with groaning, for that would be of no advantage to you."; and Proverbs 13:1states, "A wise son hears his father's instruction, but a scoffer does not listen to rebuke."

According to the Gospel of Luke, disobedience will amount to severe punishment. "And that servant who knew his master's will but did not get ready or act according to his will, will receive a severe beating. But the one who did not know, and did what deserved a beating, will receive a light beating. Everyone to whom much was given, of him much will be required, and from him to whom they entrusted much, they will demand the more." (Luke 12:47-48) In human resource management practice, this falls under insubordination. According to the Employment Act 2007, section 44, failure to obey lawful instructions leads to summary dismissal. All employees are expected to obey their supervisors and managers.

When an employee owns up to his/her mistake and apologizes, they are usually given a second chance to prove themselves. According to the book of 2 Corinthians, repentance leads to salvation whereas worldly grief produces death. "…For godly grief produces a repentance that leads to salvation without regret, whereas worldly grief produces death." (2 Corinthians 7:10) Employees are expected to perform their duties efficiently and effectively. According to the book of Proverbs, slacking in work is like relating to someone whose sole purpose is to destroy. "Whoever is slack in his work is a brother to him who destroys." (Proverbs 18:9). Proverbs 2:20-22 talks of dismissal for those that are wicked. The upright will live in the land, and the blameless will remain in it; but the wicked will be cut off from the land, and the unfaithful will be torn from it.

6.0 EMPLOYEE SEPARATION

There are different forms in which an employee can leave the organization. These include resignation, retirement, termination of contract, retrenchment, redundancy, dismissal and death. The procedure for handling the above varies depending on which form of separation it is as highlighted in the Employment Act 2007. At the point of separation, employees are to receive their rightful final dues in a timely manner. The Bible gives us a few examples of how various forms of separation were done.

When I write a response to an employee's resignation letter, I would acknowledge receipt; indicate when their last working day should be and how their final dues will be calculated upon clearance with the organization. The final dues for a resignation, for example, would be for days worked up to the last date of work; leave earned and not taken; any allowances earned as at the last date; service pay; less any debts owed to the organization. According to the book of Deuteronomy, when workers are released, they are not to be sent away empty-handed; they are to be supplied liberally from the flock, the threshing floor and your winepress. "…And when you release them, do not send them away empty-handed. Supply them liberally from your flock, your threshing floor and your winepress. Give to them as the LORD your God has blessed you." (Deuteronomy 15:13-14).

At the health facility there was a department that had many fraud cases, but when the culprits started facing summary dismissal, the fraud cases reduced. The staff in the department knew that management had its eyes on them. The book of Proverbs gives an example of a mocker being thrown out to end a fight. "Throw out the mocker, and fighting goes, too. Quarrels and insults will disappear." (Proverbs 22:10). According to the book of Revelation, the cowardly, the faithless, the detestable, as for murderers, the sexually immoral, sorcerers, idolaters, and all liars, will end up in the lake that burns with fire and sulfur. "But as for the cowardly, the faithless, the detestable, as for murderers, the sexually immoral, sorcerers, idolaters, and all liars, their portion will be in the lake that burns with fire and sulfur, which is the second death." (Revelation 21:8). The book of Ezekiel gives us another example that can be classified under dismissal. "...Behold, this was the guilt of your sister Sodom: she and her daughters had pride, excess of food, and prosperous ease, but did not aid the poor and needy. They were haughty and did an abomination before me. So I removed them, when I saw it." (Ezekiel 16:49-50).

7.0 EMPLOYEE RETENTION STRATEGIES

In order to reduce employee turnover, a human resource practitioner will need to come up with strategies that will help retain staff. There are various strategies that an organization can put in place. These include job security; training and development opportunities; career progression through succession planning; a good remuneration package; good staff welfare programs; harmonious industrial relations; and equality.

According to the book of Joshua, the Lord assured urged Joshua to be strong and courageous; to not be terrified; discouraged, for God would be with him wherever he went. This is a sense of security to have Joshua stay on course. "Have I not commanded you? Be strong and courageous. Do not be terrified; do not be discouraged, for the LORD your God will be with you wherever you go."

(Joshua 1:9). Employees will always want to work where they know they have management support. I have had a firsthand experience where my supervisors would advise that we do things a certain way and when things backfired they withdrew from the situation and left all the blame on me. I felt my job was at stake, I started looking for other jobs just in case this one would end. I have also heard many of my friends and even employees saying their supervisors have threatened to terminate their services.

The Gospel of Luke gives an example where the Lord appointed 72 followers and asked them to remain in the same house, eating and drinking whatever the owners of the house provided. He asked them not to go from house to house. This in today's world would be an advice against job hoping. Employers ought to create an environment where staffs remain committed and loyal to the organization such that we do not deal with staff replacement for those who are seeking greener pastures. "...And remain in the same house, eating and drinking what they provide, for the laborer deserves his wages. Do not go from house to house." (Luke 10:7).

Promotion is also a strategy for employee retention. In the security company, we had managers who started out as security guards then were promoted to supervisors and eventually branch managers after furthering their studies. Such managers had stayed in the company for over 25 years and you could tell their loyalty lies with the company. According to the book of Genesis, Potiphar made Joseph the overseer of his house and put him in charge of all that he had. "...Now Joseph had been brought down to Egypt, and Potiphar, an officer of Pharaoh, the captain of the guard, an Egyptian, had bought him from the Ishmaelites who had brought him down there. The Lord was with Joseph, and he became a successful man, and he was in the house of his Egyptian master. His master saw that the Lord was with him and that the Lord caused all that he did to succeed in his hands. So Joseph found favor in his sight and attended him, and he made him overseer of his house and put him in charge of all that he had. From the time that he made him overseer in his house and over all that he had the Lord blessed the Egyptian's house for Joseph's sake; the blessing of the Lord was on all that he had, in house and field . . ." (Genesis 39:1-23).

CONCLUSION

It is my hope and prayer that this book will transform the lives of many people. Students aspiring to be human resource practitioners should be encouraged to pursue this noble profession. Human resource practitioners should find comfort in the fact that the Bible, in my perspective, is indeed in support of the human resource management processes. Managers in different professions should have an eye-opening experience from this book; they should learn that there is more to human resource management than meets the eye. All organizations should embrace their employees for they are the greatest asset. It is possible to have a vision and a mission statement, but you will require people to drive 'the vehicle' towards achieving the end goal. It is high time companies invested in human capital through capacity building, good working environment, and motivation of staff. This is the very reason why human resource management as a profession is very key in all companies.

Printed in the United States
By Bookmasters